CREATING
THE FUTURE FOR
Sun Valley

CREATING THE FUTURE FOR

Sun Valley

HERITAGE, CHARM, AND A DIVERSE ECONOMY

JIMA RICE, PH.D.

Jima Rice, Ph.D.
jimasv@cox.net
or
P.O. Box 2124
Ketchum, Idaho 83340

ISBN: 978-0-578-96065-4 (Paperback)
ISBN: 978-0-578-96066-1 (eBook)

BUS068000 BUSINESS & ECONOMICS / Development / Economic Development
BUS072000 BUSINESS & ECONOMICS / Development / Sustainable Development
BUS067000 BUSINESS & ECONOMICS / Urban & Regional

Cover Designer: Zizi Iryaspraha, Pagatana Design Service, pagatana.com
Book Interior and E-book Designer: Amit Dey, amitdey2528@gmail.com
Map Designer: Evelyn Phillips, evelynphillips@me.com
Photography for front and back cover: Nils Ribi, nilsribiphotography.com
Production & Publishing Consultant: Geoff Affleck, geoffaffleck.com

For all the small business owners and entrepreneurs
who work hard to make a living in the Wood River Valley
and enrich our lives in so many ways.

Contents

Preface

reating the Future for Sun Valley reflects more than 25 years of my experiences and observations about the Wood River Valley and its approach to creating a strong economy. My perspective is based on consulting to more than 200 small businesses, entrepreneurs, non-profit organizations, and town governments, as well as simply living here and talking with others.

I moved to the Valley to run rivers in 1992 as a location-neutral entrepreneur working with a Boston-based management consulting firm whose corporate clients represented a wide range of industries. Soon, I added a local consulting practice to my work. One early client, the Sun Valley/Ketchum Chamber of Commerce, hired me to facilitate their annual retreat. It was there that I first learned how much leaders of the business community deferred to Sun Valley Resort and its tourism interests in making decisions about what was best for the local community and its quality of life.

Over the next few years, my experiences with other Valley clients broadened my views of the local economy. Most of the small business owners I worked with provided everyday goods and services to locals, second homeowners, and tourists alike without making any distinction between them, other than how easy they were to work with or whether they paid their bills on time.

I began wondering why the tourist paradigm dominated marketing efforts when it seemed that the entire small business sector drove the economy and gave the Valley much of its flavor. Tourism was just one niche within it. Indeed, the presence of so many varied small businesses with their clapboard and brick storefronts, friendly owners, and long histories was a central part of the Valley's unique charm. Rather than focus solely on attracting visitors, it seemed more sensible to build a year-round economy of diverse businesses in the interests of economic stability, maintaining close community ties, and providing a more interesting texture to the Valley's already envious quality of life.

Over the years, I watched many false starts to building local economic strength, perhaps due to a lack of local expertise about economic development and personal business interests that were undermining the Valley's quality of life. Through it all, the tourism mantra prevailed, to the detriment, I believe, of the Valley's future. That conclusion led me to write this book, using my knowledge, research, conversations, and business background to shape my perspective.

A few caveats are important. In a small community, where someone you haven't seen in a couple of months can tell you what you've been doing for the past few weeks, providing the name of anyone referred to or quoted in these pages would distract from substantive points. So, I've avoided most names, whether of elected leaders, agency heads, well-known locals, or those who've trusted me enough to share their personal thoughts. Nevertheless, a few can be identified by their roles in Valley life, but that was unavoidable to tell the tale.

Since, in casual conversation, a comment about "Sun Valley" can mean the City of Sun Valley, Sun Valley Resort, the north Wood River Valley or, more generally and more frequently, the entire Wood River Valley, I've tried to make my references specific.

Throughout the book, the words "entrepreneur," "small business owner," "Main Street," and "small businesses" are used interchangeably. Years ago, "entrepreneur" referred to someone starting a business in the technology industry. Today, the media and everyday conversation use all four terms to signify the small business owners at the center of America's economy: the persistent, independent, passionate risk-takers who have identified a "problem" or "need" that they are sure they can resolve. They are the movers and shakers who fuel the economy.

Finally, much of what I have written is an amalgam of information from books, interviews, articles, casual comments, observation, and internet sources. I've learned about Western history and, especially, the Wood River Valley's past and present. I've learned about entrepreneurship, too. When I first began to work locally in the 1990s, I had been consulting with national corporations. After facilitating the Sun Valley/Ketchum Chamber of Commerce retreat, I began to pay more attention to the nature of the local economy. Then, I began to realize that my clients, large or small, were all entrepreneurs. As I began to advocate supporting Main Street, I was often drawn into politics that opposed what I was doing, but the encounters only further confirmed my impressions.

Faced by contradictory anecdotes, data, or other information, I've considered the historical and social context, sought additional references, talked to knowing locals, and used common sense to decide what to include. But errors may have slipped by in my reliance on multiple sources. What I've written here captures my views and interpretation of situations and events for which only I am responsible. I have tried to be fair and welcome any verifiable corrections.

My major sources are cited in the Endnotes and Bibliography. I think all of them are well worth reading for the far more complete picture they present. Otherwise, topics of interest to the reader can easily be researched on the Internet.

My email, should you wish to reach me with questions, information, or corrections is jimasv@cox.net.

The Big Picture

S et in post-Civil War California, Clint Eastwood's 1985 spare, black-and-white film, *Pale Rider* (shot in the Wood River Valley), portrays the early years of the mining industry. A group of tin-pan miners and their families are working the small mountain streams of the Sierra Nevada for gold when the owner of a large hydraulic mining company shows up. He wants to monopolize the area's mineral deposits and directs his thugs to force the miners off the land through threats and violence, including killing a little girl's dog. A lone cowboy, a stranger played by Eastwood, rides in from the far hills and quietly, almost wordlessly, takes up residence. He is soon called Preacher because of the clerical collar he wears.

By the end of the film, after several harrowing incidents, the company owner, his thugs, and six corrupt sheriff's deputies have been killed in gun fights. The miners and their town have been saved. His work done, Preacher rides alone toward the distant horizon with a young girl's loving "Thanks" echoing after him. Paul Smith, author of *Clint Eastwood: A Cultural Production,* explains the film's starkly presented moral: "(A) small community of independent miners is preferable to the technologized corporation exactly because it is a community (and a) virtuous and self-sufficient community is simply better for the land."[1]

Pale Rider had one of the highest-grossing box office receipts for any Western in the 1980s. Perhaps it was because so many communities in the United States, mining and otherwise, had become economically dependent on one industrial company owned by one man or one syndicate, often with harmful consequences for the town's employees, environment, quality of life, and long-term prosperity.

Most of these towns, stripped of their natural resources and located in narrow mountainous terrain, were useless for further industrial operations. They became economically depressed and many became ghost towns.[2] In the 1930s, however, a few aspiring entrepreneurs realized that the snow blanketing the mountains around their towns was an economic asset. All they had to do was mount a rope tow on a snowy hill and people would show up for a few runs.

Eventually, while some ski areas stayed small, others expanded into larger, often fancier vacation resorts and, by the 1980s, skiing had become big business. In the 1990s, however, Baby Boom ski enthusiasts began to slow down, ski operations had become ever more expensive, and new kinds of adventurous vacations were available. The industry's subsequent struggles caught the attention of private investor groups that saw opportunities in fixed assets, cash flow, and, most important, surrounding land for private development, using skiing as a loss leader. These groups bought one resort, and then another and another, gathering them under one corporate umbrella for commercialized branding and mass marketing, offering discount packages that covered everything from airfare to lodging to ski rental, to keep visitors at the resort from arrival to departure. In the process, local community life was altered, its histories and traditions reshaped or vastly diluted.[3]

The Wood River Valley, itself an historic mining area, had better luck. It was neither ruinously exploited by the mining industry, nor gobbled up by a private equity group. In 1936, it became the home of Sun Valley Resort, the country's first destination ski area, owned successively and without interruption for the next eighty years by three wealthy entrepreneurial men who loved the Valley and operated the Resort as much for their personal pride and pleasure as for profit. Thus, the Valley was able to keep intact for decades much of its original Western heritage, authenticity, and friendly, small-town feel: a quality of life that one might call the Valley's "brand."

This book presents my view of Sun Valley Resort's impact on the Wood River Valley over the last eighty years and the community's adaptations to that impact. It seems as if the two were in a dance, with the Resort initially leading the community's growth until, gradually, the small business economy began to create its own dance steps and become more of an equal partner. Today, the community's economy has a wide range of successful business niches, with tourism only one of them. Yet, tourism remains the dominant promotion and marketing focus, mostly driven by government officials and a real estate lobby that favors the construction of expensive second homes and commercial projects, despite how they have been altering the Valley's lifestyle for the past two decades.

Fortunately, there is still time to pursue a more enlightened strategy to strengthen, expand, and diversify our economy. Tourism clearly plays an important role, but so do all other Main Street niches, and they should not be ignored. According to studies described later in this book, a diverse entrepreneurial culture would render the economy more resilient, sustainable, and vital. It would help to preserve the Valley's heritage and authentic lifestyle so beloved by everyone, whether locals, second homeowners, or vacationers passing through.

History shows that it is entrepreneurship that laid the foundation for America's greatness and has served as both the backbone and beating heart of America's culture. In the 1800s, it was the driven and persistent efforts of inventors whose products required automated manufacturing that led to America's industrial revolution. Entrepreneurs created the mom-and-pop businesses that lined Main Streets across America. Today's technology mega-businesses once were start-ups, powered by the clever founders of Microsoft, Apple, and Amazon.

Perhaps it is time for the Valley to follow the entrepreneurial bent of our Resort owners, and of the country. Rather than marketing just tourism, let's market our entrepreneurial past, as well as present and future. Let's be the leader of destination resorts in building a diverse small business culture that ensures the economic stability many of them lack. Let's emphasize that preserving our community lifestyle, with its enduring social and business ties, is our vision. Let's show how deeply American we are, upholding the core values of individualism, personal enterprise, and humanism.

If the community were able to reach a consensus favoring an entrepreneurial future for the Valley, *Pale Rider's* message could then reverberate across the hills with just a few changes: "A small community of independent business owners pursuing their dreams is preferable to relying on one dominant business or industry. In the long run, a virtuous, economically diverse, and self-sufficient community is simply better for the land and the well-being of its people."

PART I

THE RESORT

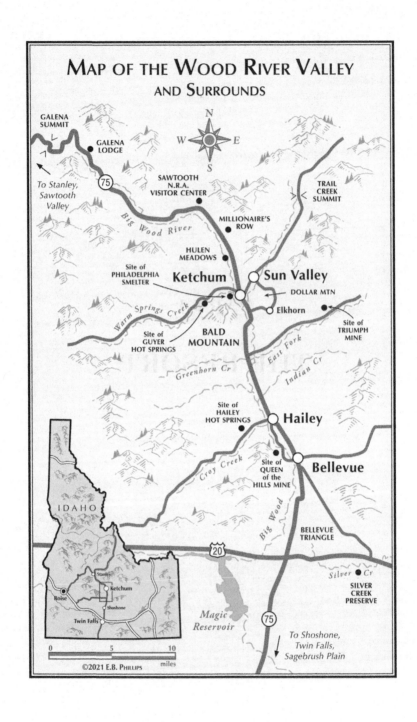

MAP OF THE WOOD RIVER VALLEY
AND SURROUNDS

GALENA
SUMMIT

GALENA
LODGE

N
W E
S

To Stanley,
Sawtooth
Valley

75

SAWTOOTH
N.R.A.
VISITOR CENTER

TRAIL
CREEK
SUMMIT

Big Wood River

MILLIONAIRE'S
ROW

HULEN
MEADOWS

Site of
PHILADELPHIA
SMELTER

Ketchum

Sun Valley

DOLLAR MTN

Warm Springs Creek

Elkhorn

Site of
TRIUMPH
MINE

Site of
GUYER
HOT SPRINGS

BALD
MOUNTAIN

East Fork

Indian Cr

Greenhorn Cr

Site of
HAILEY
HOT SPRINGS

Hailey

Croy Creek

Site of
QUEEN
of the
HILLS MINE

Bellevue

IDAHO

Big Wood

BELLEVUE
TRIANGLE

20

Silver Cr

SILVER
CREEK
PRESERVE

Stanley

Ketchum

Boise

Shoshone

Twin Falls

Magic
Reservoir

75

To Shoshone,
Twin Falls,
Sagebrush Plain

0   5   10
miles

©2021 E.B. PHILLIPS

Chapter One[4]

Before Fame and Fortune

*"The present was an egg laid by the past that had
the future inside its shell."*

—Zora Neale Hurston

In the early days of American settlement, the Wood River Valley
had characteristics that were advantageous to people seeking a prosperous life in the West: expansive beauty and diverse wildlife; vast
territory open for settlement; mineral resources; hot springs, plentiful
game, and fish-rich rivers. Eventually, irrigation would open thousands
of acres for agriculture and animal husbandry. The interplay of these
elements over time laid down the history that the Valley carries today
in its blood and bones. It is what we have inherited as a community,
consciously and unconsciously. It is a history worth some review before
we go forward to Sun Valley Resort days.

Native American Times

Conventional wisdom has it that the glories of the West were discovered by the first white men to see them, just as Columbus is said to

have "discovered" America. As with all American history, however, the European settlement of America was just a dot in time compared with the earliest Idahoans who first appeared approximately fourteen thousand years ago, pursuing the woolly mammoth and great bison. From the earth-centered perspective of these indigenous peoples, places were not "discovered;" they had simply been there for a long, long time and, with proper care and appreciation, their beauties and bounty would last far into the future. (Evidence of Native American activity going back 10,000 years has been found in stone artifacts at Elkhorn Village in the City of Sun Valley.)[5]

Of the many Native American tribes in Idaho, the Shoshoni and Bannock lived in the Wood River Valley region, moving in small bands from camp to camp along the floor of the Big Wood River Valley according to food availability and weather, traveling the same trails used by migrating wildlife. The native peoples lived off the land: hunting, fishing, and collecting seeds and bulbs in high mountain meadows during the summer and traveling into the lower, more salutary prairies when winter came. Remnants of tribal encampments and daily life are scattered throughout the Valley.

Native American values could not have been more different from those of the settlers about to sweep into their homeland. The tribal culture was communal and egalitarian, headed by chiefs admired for their bravery and generosity. The land was part of oneself, the repository of spirits and historic artifacts that influenced the present. It was an inheritance to be honored and passed on forever. As the Iroquois Nation wrote in its Constitution, "Look and listen for the welfare of the whole people and have always in view not only the present but also the coming generations, even those whose faces are yet beneath the surface of the ground — the unborn of the future Nation."[6]

This lifestyle contrasted with the settlers' encroaching capitalist culture in which land was sold for profit and natural resources exploited at the direction of military and government officials, businessmen and land planners, lawyers and financiers, all for the sake of what was called "Manifest Destiny," the belief that God intended American civilization with its "exceptional" settlers (compared to so-called "inferior" indigenous tribes) to spread culture and a particular economic system across the continent.

Settlers Come on the Scene

The first major commercial endeavor in the Pacific Northwest was harvesting animal pelts. In 1824, a Scottish fur trader named Alexander Ross, employed by Canada's Hudson's Bay Company (still in operation), was the first white man to explore the Big Wood River Valley. Ross is credited with "discovering" Galena Summit, home of the Big Wood River's headwaters that flowed south into the Valley basin. (An interpretive sign announcing his discovery — and offering a spectacular view of the Stanley Basin — lies just south of the summit.)

Ross was one of the so-called "mountain men." Some were lone trappers; others, like Ross, had corporate employers. They roamed the rugged Northwest Coast and inland areas, dependent for their livelihoods on collecting beaver skins and other furs popular in America and Europe. Farthest from their minds was founding settlements. In fact, the Hudson's Bay Company directed its trappers to practice a scorched earth policy to deter competitors who might follow behind. Nevertheless, Ross and his contemporaries laid down trails that opened the wilderness. And they befriended Native Americans with whom they formed collaborative trading networks benefitting East and West Coast fur-trading companies. Indifferent to sustaining the land's resources, however, trappers nearly eliminated the region's beaver population by 1850. Fortunately for the beaver, European fashion began to favor silk. So ended the first corporate business activity in the Wood River Valley.

The mountain men were followed by an ever-widening stream of American citizens and immigrants seeking economic opportunity and personal freedom in the West's wide-open spaces. In 1841, the first small band of settlers left Independence, Missouri for the West. Just two years later, a group of 1,000 settlers driving more than 100 large-wheeled wagons and leading 5,000 oxen and cattle, left Elm Grove, Missouri for Oregon, headed West on what became known as the Oregon Trail, a journey of 2,170 miles. (When continental rail travel emerged in 1869, the flow of wagon trains diminished and, by 1890, the Oregon Trail had been eclipsed). Once settled, many ambitious and hard-working pioneers began to log the Northwest's old-growth forests for timber and dig into its earth for the surface and ground minerals needed by America's industrializing cities.

Thar's Gold in Them Thar Hills

The second economic bounty found in the West, far more valuable than beaver skins, was gold, discovered in California in 1848. The rush for the ore that cannot be destroyed by water, time, or fire — and has the most appeal to the human eye — was on. Thousands of pioneers streamed West over the Oregon Trail, many to prospect for the glittering substance and get rich, others to build towns, ranches, farms, and businesses to meet the daily needs of sprouting mining communities. Wherever gold and other ore deposits were found, small towns mushroomed overnight and remained for as long as the resource held out.

In 1862, central Idaho, especially the land around the Boise Basin, claimed its own gold rush. Settlers flooded what was still a territory in 1863 and mining soon anchored the Boise area economy. Anyone seeking a potentially sound financial future might find it by simply digging into unexplored ground. That same year, President Lincoln passed the Homestead Act to further encourage Western develop-ment, permitting adults who had never borne arms against the United States, including freed slaves, to settle 160 acres of federally owned and surveyed land. A homesteader had to meet just three requirements to become a property owner: build a 12' x 14' home, cultivate the land for five years, and pay a small registration fee.

The next year, Lincoln passed the Pacific Railway Act to begin construction of a transcontinental railroad that would provide faster, more efficient access to the West. Soon, the Union Pacific and Central Pacific railroads, spurred by government incentives, were laying track toward each other from their respective East and West coasts. The two tracks ultimately converged in 1869 in Promontory, Utah and were joined with a ceremonial golden spike that signified the economic and strategic importance of transcontinental travel. (The Central Pacific was owned by Leland Stanford and the spike now rests at Stanford University).

With the railroad in place, raw and finished goods, and enterprising people began to flow back and forth across the country. Financing was often available from a cadre of East Coast tycoons, eager to invest in the railroad, mining, and timber industries. Many of them were the so-called robber barons — J.P. Morgan, E.H. Harriman, Andrew Carnegie, Jay Gould, and John D. Rockefeller — who eagerly extended their long-armed control over industries, towns, and politics everywhere they did business. Whether trying to appeal to these industrialists or not, the Federal Government passed the General Mining Act in 1872, incenting individuals, companies, and international corporations to head West where they could patent one acre of mineral-rich land for $2.50-$5.00 and extract what lay beneath it for free.

In 1879, the Wood River Valley finally found its own rich deposits of lead-silver ore (called galena), along with a few gold deposits, and joined the mining world with hundreds of individual claims staked in the Valley where many of their remnants are still visible.[7] A couple of years later, John Hailey and several friends platted the City of Hailey in the South Valley as the center of trade and transportation to support mining, the growth of agriculture, and the influx of people seeking prosperous lives in a booming, if hard to reach, area. The most intensive mining started in Hailey's Broadford area where, for the next decade, the Minnie Moore, Queen of the Hills, and other mines produced $60 million of silver-lead ore (roughly $1.5 billion today). Hailey became a boom town, the County seat, and the first city in the Northwest to have electric lights.

Soon, Philadelphia moneymen stepped forward with $2 million ($51.3 million today) to fund the Philadelphia Mining and Smelting Company.[8] Smelting was expensive but refining the Valley's heavy ores on site would reduce their out-bound transportation costs. The operation opened in 1882 on 160-acres in the City of Ketchum's Warm Springs area with ore furnaces, barns, two 40-ton smelting furnaces, offices, bunkhouses, mess halls, and a large community of miners, office workers, and managers. The output from Valley mines grew to over $1 million annually ($25.5 million today), much of which was refined at the smelter which, hour after hour, generated charcoal heat to separate lead and silver ores from their sulfide components. Admired for its size and productivity, the smelter was the largest employer in the Valley, "doing more to develop the Valley than any five mining companies." The silver it yielded went for roughly $30 per ounce (just under $800 today).

Speculative capital began to pour into the Valley from investors in Salt Lake City, the Midwest, and even London, looking for big financial returns from new and expanding mining companies that were regularly bought and sold at ever rising prices. Local commerce burgeoned, as did a more exciting lifestyle, according to reports of the day. Baseball fans could travel cheaply and reliably to Shoshone for games on a new railroad spur! Whiskey was said to be more abundant than water, and, despite an increasingly settled social environment, effective law enforcement was often non-existent. Most valuable of all, the Valley no longer shut down completely during the winter; its population and economy continued to function, albeit at a slower pace, hanging on until spring.

Native Lands Pass into Settler Ownership

During these decades of American settlement, the vast number of Native American tribes struggled, having little chance against the combined juggernaut of ambitious European settlers, industrial development, and a laissez-faire capitalist economy backed by the United States government and military. The tribes' lifestyle of living sustainably and in spiritual partnership with the land was challenged, denigrated and, with surprising speed, nearly destroyed. Buffalo populations were decimated, and ancient lands were seized. In 1855, the United States began ordering Native American tribes onto reservations and, just a decade later, Indian lands across the West were put up for sale to settlers. The direction of fourteen thousand years of history was changed forever in a short span of five decades to fulfill America's conviction that it had been called by God to spread its economic system and His special blessings across America.

In 1881, after owners of the Idaho and Oregon Land Improvement Company were tipped off by Union Pacific friends about a planned Oregon Short Line rail spur from Shoshone to Hailey, momentum to buy newly available land in the Valley took off. When the spur was completed in 1883, resource extraction intensified. Now, ores could more quickly reach far-off urban centers and feed their industrial operations. When the trains returned, they brought back heavy equipment, domestic products, and more new settlers.

Growth boomed between 1880 and 1890 as acreage was sold to ranchers and farmers, hoteliers, immigrants, miners, wholesalers, commercial entrepreneurs, and other community builders. Finally, in June 1890, the year Idaho became a state, the 11th United States Census declared the disappearance of the American frontier on the grounds that all land tracts measuring at least one square mile were inhabited by two or more settlers.

At that point, Hailey and Bellevue constituted one of the most populated areas in Idaho territory, worthy of four newspapers to inform the several thousand residents.[9] In 1882, the Wood River Times was established (and published until 1915), a daily newspaper that provided articles on political, entertainment, and community events (such as the "tantrum" thrown by Bellevue's postmaster when he refused to deliver mail for eight hours), notices for the arrival of special items like a "Chicago Organ," and advertisements by small businesses meeting the needs of the time: grocery and hardware stores; medical and legal professionals; assayers and surveyors; blacksmiths and liveries; purveyors of mining supplies; and liquor and lumber stores. Saloons and gambling establishments were especially popular: in 1884, the sheriff issued licenses to 18 saloon keepers and 12 gambling establishments in Hailey, and another 18 saloons and 2 breweries in Bellevue.

Unfortunately, the International Silver Depression began in 1888 and silver prices crashed, hitting their lowest in the Panic of 1893 when railroads, banks, and businesses across the country failed. The Philadelphia Smelter closed, the Valley's mining towns shrank, and the area's population dwindled to roughly 2,500, one-quarter of what it had been before the Silver Depression.

Economic conditions and the finite resources of an extractive industry like mining inevitably ordain its decline and mining became mostly quiescent in the mid-1890s, having lasted just 10-15 years. Only the Triumph and Queen of the Hills mines continued, the former closing in 1957 (leaving behind toxic waste deposits) and the latter running until 1970.

Hail the Hot Springs

After the mining economy failed, the populations of Bellevue, Hailey, and Ketchum stood at 892, 1,073, and 465. Valley residents faced serious economic hardships as a one-industry Valley. But times were changing in the West. With Native Americans removed to reservations and rail travel continually expanding, the once forbidding West was seen as increasingly safe and accessible. Western settlement gained speed, particularly as the wilderness preservation movement developed. Romanticized through poetry, art, and fiction, preservationists characterized the West as the architect of the American character — spirited, innovative, and inspired.[10] It was the symbol of America as a distinct and proud new country, a place to re-establish oneself, find prosperity, and spread "civilization." An 1872 painting, "American Progress" by John Gast, captures the attitude of the times. It depicts settlers flooding out of a light-filled East across open lands toward the dark skies of the West, led by the heavenly lady, "Columbia," who signifies civilization. Before them, fleeing across the open lands, run Native Americans and buffalo.[11]

The Wood River Valley's atmosphere evolved into one of progress, risk, and adventure. It was perfect for starting over, for trying something new. Moreover, in the late 1870s, Americans had begun to emulate the European health practice of "taking the waters" — drinking and bathing in hot springs — of which the Valley had plenty. In 1879, the Croy family, owners of land with thermal waters up a Hailey side canyon, opened the "Hailey Hot Springs" for paid public access — as other spa towns were doing across America.

A decade later, a Valley newcomer, land developer, and one-time publicist for Union Pacific, John Strahorn, bought the Croy hot springs and an adjacent 1,000-acre ranch. On that enlarged site he built a luxurious colonial-style hotel, a few small cabins, and a hospital. The Hailey Hot Springs Hotel opened in 1888 with a spectacular ball and was soon hosting 50-100 guests each day. Praise abounded for its hot and cold plunges, steam baths for ladies and gentlemen, billiard and bar rooms, parlors, and music rooms.[12] The Wood River Times cooed, "The visitors to the springs were not of the eastern penny-pinching class of tourists…They were usually very wealthy people, who demanded the best there was to be had, expecting to pay well for it. It is estimated that they put into circulation in this immediate vicinity between $300 and $500 a day."

The Hailey Hot Springs were not without competition, however. In 1887, the equally fashionable Guyer Hot Springs opened in the North Valley, near what is now Baldy's Warm Springs base. It, too, offered plush accommodations for the wealthy vacationer: a restaurant and bar, a dozen rooms, a bathhouse, a ladies' parlor, and a 20-foot by 40-foot dance floor. The daily scene was robust: "Guyer Hotel guests enjoyed hot and cold water in their rooms, an open-air plunge, and bathing facilities separated for the sexes...Local ladies wore plumed hats and sixteen-button gloves while they played tennis or croquet, swung on a big wooden swing, and danced in the pavilions...Women splashed in long pantaloons and dresses."

One of Guyer Hot Springs' better-known visitors was the robber baron, Jay Gould. Although living on New York City's Fifth Avenue with his family, he had invested in Hailey's Red Elephant mine and other distant ventures. Curious about the Wood River Valley, he boarded his private train for Guyer Hot Springs and arrived in the summer of 1891. Although Gould was nationally reviled for his greedy manipulation of Wall Street, one of the Valley's liberally-minded newspapers described him as less of a "Wall Street terror" than a man with the talent to exploit an already "damnable system." While his family relaxed, Gould fished for trout and, upon returning to his friends on Wall Street, reported that the fishing was the finest he had ever experienced.

Other East Coast businessmen visited in Gould's wake and reports spread about the Valley's abundant hunting and fishing, luxurious hot springs, and magnificent setting. By 1914, Guyer Hot Springs was well-known and had expanded to include a lovely first-class, two-story hotel, including electricity, that reputedly became "one of the famous hot springs of the west." Resort tourism had conquered the Valley for the first time, but not the last.

Baa, Baa, Baa

As the Wood River Valley's population and economy rose and fell with beaver harvesting, ore mining, and hot springs tourism, yet a fourth industry grew steadily in the background: sheep ranching. The woolly animals were first brought to the Valley by John Hailey in the 1860s with timing that was either fortuitous or prescient. The Civil War soon broke out and wool's inherent durability, insulation, and resistance to fire and water made it ideal for soldiers' uniforms, blankets (for horses and humans), and tents.

After the war, the Valley's sheep industry continued to grow, soon reaching over 600,000 in number. Scottish and Basque sheepherders trailed bands of 1,500-2,500 animals twice a year from summer pasture in the Boulder, Pioneer, and Sawtooth Mountains to winter pasture on the Snake River Plain. The animals grew healthy, browsing the open rangeland in the dry air they liked so much, while herders passed the time carving their initials on Aspen tree trunks. The industry thrived as new freight lines carried sheep to Midwestern distribution terminals in Omaha, Chicago, and Kansas City. By 1918, Idaho's sheep population had reached 2,650,000, six sheep for every human, and over the next 30 years, Ketchum became the West's largest sheep shipping center. It was not until the 1970s that the local human-sheep ratio finally pulled even.

Seasonal sheepherding continues through the Valley today and is honored each fall by the Trailing of the Sheep festival when bands of sheep run down Main Street accompanied by sheepherders, their herding border collies, and Great Pyrenees guard dogs.

A New Horizon

Even before the Great Depression arrived, the first three of the Wood River Valley's major income-producing industries were no longer viable. They had depended on outside corporate financing (no longer available), plentiful resources (substantially depleted), and tourists on trains (now drawn to the novelty of automobile and airplane travel). The previous influx of settlers had disappeared and much of the business community with it. The sheep business was still thriving, but its earnings could not support the local economy.

The Valley was at a low ebb. But then, something entirely unexpected happened and the Valley's situation began to change in a big way. It was 1936 and an East Coast financier named Averell Harriman came to the rugged, wide-open town of Ketchum and changed the Valley's future forever.

Wise Visionary: W. Averell Harriman

"Ski resorts might become a much-needed
new industry in the mountain states."

—Averell Harriman

In 1936, W. Averell Harriman was a 45-year-old East Coast business magnate, a man with vision and a strong entrepreneurial drive. Among his many and diverse holdings were the Union Pacific Railroad, two Wall Street banks, Russian mines, cargo ships, and polo ponies. A Board Director of more than 40 companies, he was one of the more influential men of his time. Coincidentally, he had also spent much of his youth in the West, in Idaho on a ranch near Yellowstone, and was comfortable in mountains, forests, and fields.

Harriman's Background

Averell Harriman's father, E.H. Harriman, was a ruthless businessman, one of the robber barons who, over forty years, built a transportation empire that reached around the world. After Union Pacific went bankrupt in the Panic of 1893, Harriman bought it and built it into the largest, most efficient monopoly rail conglomerate in U.S. history. At one point, he owned so many railroads and steamship lines that, traveling on his own properties, he could steam from New York to New Orleans, ride the rails west to San Francisco, steam to China and back, and return to the East Coast on an entirely different railroad. It was Harriman's business practices that helped motivate President Theodore Roosevelt to "bust the trusts," breaking up corporate monopolies that restrained trade and manipulated markets.

When Harriman died in 1909, he left his capable and socially minded wife, Mary, a $150-$200 million estate, the largest fortune in America. His son, Averell, just 17 years old and about to enter Yale, inherited his dad's seat on Union Pacific's board and received significant railroad stock from his mother. Whether his father would have thought Averell ready for such responsibility is hard to say. E.H. kept a close and demanding eye on his son, constantly complaining about his mediocre academic performance at Groton, a Massachusetts prep school, and believing that Averell cared more about football than grades. Harriman wanted Averell to be responsible, aim high, work hard, and make a name for himself doing great things to benefit society.

In the long run, Averell would likely have impressed his father, proving to be an energetic, ambitious, and creative businessman with varied interests, high scruples, and sensitivity to the human condition. It was this man who stepped into the sleepy, sheep-shipping center of the Wood River Valley to build the first destination ski resort in the United States in the wilderness heart of the virtually unknown state of Idaho.

Before that moment, Averell had been busy honing his business skills, building his financial portfolio, and establishing his reputation. After graduation, the young scion had interned at Union Pacific, working on the tracks with labor gangs, and rotating through various departments. The company's President, impressed by Harriman's work ethic and abilities, gave him a special assignment to identify sources of waste in the railroad's operations. Alert to efficiency and the bottom line, Harriman did well. At the end of the year, he was elevated to Junior Vice-President for purchasing in charge of a $50,000,000 budget. One of his first steps was to end the long-standing collusive bidding among suppliers, immediately improving the railroad's bottom line.

Harriman clearly could have continued to work at Union Pacific but office administration wasn't in his nature. He had a hungry mind and was restless and energetic. Nor was he afraid to work hard, believing that even the wealthiest had a duty to be productive, rather than waste time in selfish pursuits. An entrepreneur to the bone, he could not help but hunt for new business opportunities. When World War I began and America and Britain began to defensively expand worldwide shipping, Harriman resigned from Union Pacific and borrowed money from his mother to create the Merchant Shipbuilding Corporation at a deteriorating shipyard on Pennsylvania's Delaware River. Building merchant ships to transport needed materials to England would be his war service, rather than enlisting (much to the scorn of several service-bound friends).

Working with a team of creative designers, Harriman instituted a new approach to shipbuilding — manufacturing prefabricated steel panels that could be quickly assembled. Although the first ships were not ready until the Armistice, Harriman's efforts, together with others, made America the world leader in shipbuilding by 1918. Harriman was just 27. Next, he worked to create a worldwide shipping fleet (echoes of his father) and was successful enough to be called "The Steamship King." By 1925, however, his efforts had failed for a variety of reasons, including a post-War glut of shipbuilding that collapsed the industry and forced him to search for other business opportunities.

While he was busy building ships, Harriman also founded the banking firm of W.A. Harriman and Company in 1920, followed a few years later by a second bank, Harriman Brothers & Company, founded with his brother, Roland. The banks financed Harriman's forays into Russian manganese mines, Silesian coal mines, and Polish zinc and steel, some of which were successful and some that were not. At the height of the Depression in 1931, Harriman Brothers merged with the eminent but equally distressed, Brown Brothers & Co. to become the still operating banking powerhouse of Brown Brothers Harriman. Harriman was also an inveterate speculator in aviation, newspapers, and horse racing (trotters and thoroughbreds). In the long run, though, he proved most successful at international diplomacy and banking.

Revitalizing Union Pacific

By 1932, Union Pacific had been catering to the tourist trade for nearly a decade as the Utah Parks Commission, a concessionaire with the National Parks Service, and had built hotels and operated rail and bus lines for vacationers eager to explore the wonders of the newly opened West: the Grand Canyon, Zion, and Bryce National Parks. But automobiles and airplanes had begun to attract travelers with their greater speed, independence, and mobility, reducing Union Pacific's passenger travel by a notable twenty-four percent.

As Board Chair, Harriman decided to take a first-hand look at what it was like to ride his trains. On a field trip, he walked from his comfortable personal car to the passenger section. There he found empty, noisy, badly appointed cars, indifferent customer service, and barely edible food. Since the federal government still required passenger service, Harriman faced two options: restore quality passenger travel or let it continue to drain the railroad's income. He chose the former path but went beyond simple restoration to invent something new and dramatic: the Streamliner, a state-of-the-art, sleek, fast

18

luxury train that echoed the aerodynamic design of airplanes and automobiles but offered a more comfortable, and affordable, way to travel to far-off places.

The first Streamliner, introduced in 1934, was the M-10000, nicknamed "Little Zip." It was beautiful. A smooth, oval-nosed engine painted canary yellow and chocolate brown pulled lightweight, tubular Art Deco cars with upholstered tilting seats, air conditioning, and tasty food. Friendly attendants met every customer need. Powered by the new diesel fuel, Little Zip could travel an unheard-of 100+ miles per hour over long distances – meaning lower operating costs for Union Pacific and lower ticket prices for passengers.

Harriman's invention was branded "Tomorrow's Train Today," and it attracted such a large following that Harriman upgraded his older, clunkier trains with wake-up calls by stewardesses, tasty food, puffed pillows, and air conditioning, all at an affordable ticket price. He renamed the refurbished trains the Challenger line and it became Union Pacific's most profitable division for passenger travel until it was retired in 1971.

The Birth and Development of Sun Valley

Harriman's "build it and they will come" attitude soon tacked in another direction that could increase Union Pacific income. Although not a skier, Harriman was familiar with European ski resorts from his business travels and friends who vacationed abroad. He also knew that the 1932 Lake Placid Olympics had introduced Americans to skiing and they had fallen in love with it. European travel was beyond most budgets, however, and Harriman watched as mountain areas near cities began to offer weekend recreational skiing. Harriman soon imagined a relaxed, comfortable journey on the Little Zip across the United States to a lovely mountain resort built for his wealthy friends. The get-away spot would be unique in its solitude, and luxurious enough for society's elite to visit for several days to ski, dine, and enjoy the outdoors. He had envisioned America's first "destination ski resort," far more accessible than the usual week-long ocean crossing to Europe followed by a train ride into the Alps.

To some, Harriman's vision might have seemed a shot in the dark by a foolhardy man with too much money. But he was neither rash nor a spendthrift, neither impractical nor a self-indulgent skier. He was a serious businessman who set about making the case for Union Pacific to fund the deal, commissioning a market study from no less than the United States Assistant Secretary of Commerce. The results showed growing sales of ski clothing, equipment, and accessories both at home and abroad. Another study described the new ski areas as "generally unsatisfactory," offering nothing more than a crowded weekend get-away, not the gracious experience that Harriman had in mind.

Writing to Union Pacific's President, Carl Gray, Harriman described America's growing taste for skiing but the lack of high-quality resorts that could attract discriminating guests for long vacations. He proposed to initiate "long haul" tourist travel to a new ski resort in the West, wryly noting to Gray that, at last, there would be good reason to travel through snow fields that periodically blocked trains along their routes. Harriman even went so far as to predict that his proposed "destination" ski resort might inaugurate a new industry for the Northwest.

To most city folk at the time, the West was far away, perhaps even frightening, but for Harriman, the West was deeply familiar. In his teens, he had cut down brush and trees to help lay Union Pacific tracks in Montana. When he was twenty years old, his mother had bought property in Island Park, Idaho, a beautiful drainage basin on the Snake River Plateau. There, on the Henry's Fork of the Snake River at his family's "Railroad Ranch," Harriman had enjoyed fishing, hunting, and relaxing on thousands of acres of lush, wide open country. (The ranch is now a public park).[14]

Gray was persuaded and gave Harriman the go-ahead to build the resort, stipulating that Union Pacific would own and finance it only if losses remained below $1,000,000 per year (roughly $19,000,000 in today's dollars). Harriman immediately got to work. He had once met a young Austrian chamois hunting in Europe and, when the man's parents asked Harriman to teach their son some responsibility, he had brought him to New York City to work as a clerk. The young man, Count Felix Von Schaffgotsch, was back in Austria but delighted to return for Harriman's assignment: Locate the perfect out-of-the-way mountain site for a ski resort to match those in Europe. The site had to be near an existing Union Pacific route but too far for a short weekend jaunt by hordes of city people in automobiles. It should have a sunny, dry climate with just the right amount of snow for good skiing, specifically "not too wet or too much of it."[15] Given that Harriman did not yet ski, one wonders how he got such a good fix on what a resort should provide.

Schaffgotsch's assignment might have overwhelmed another young man, but not him. Dashing, energetic, and intrepid, he traveled 7,000 miles in six weeks to explore roughly 20 possible resort venues, none of which satisfied him. He was ready to return to New York City when, sharing drinks with some locals in a Boise, Idaho bar, he learned about the Wood River Valley and an outpost there named Ketchum. The dying sheep-shipping town (population 100-200) could be reached by Union Pacific's Oregon Short Line which ran from Shoshone to Hailey three times a week. The Count immediately headed to Shoshone, arriving in a snowstorm that blocked train service. Undeterred, he cajoled a local to drive him the rest of the way. The two slid into a snowdrift but miraculously found a snowplow to follow into Hailey. There the Count caught a bus to Ketchum and made friends with a fellow passenger, Roberta Brass, the friendly daughter of a Ketchum sheep rancher.

Schaffgotsch's persistence was rewarded when he arrived in Ketchum. That winter had brought an unusually bountiful 10 feet of snow. After a few days skiing around the Valley on one of his five pairs of skis – following a young boy on long wooden slats – the Count felt he had found Harriman's "perfect" spot. The hills and an inviting mountain (Bald Mountain) were covered with feathery snow; the Valley was a windless, sunlit pocket that held the sun's warmth. The area was breathtakingly beautiful. Locals reported that the warmest spot in the Valley was the ranch owned by Roberta Brass' father, lying in a protected cup of land where the sun shone 80% of the time. The Count immediately wired Harriman: "Among the many attractive spots I have visited, this combined more delightful features than any other place I have seen in the U.S., Switzerland, or Austria for a winter sports center."

With Schaffgotsch on the prowl, Harriman decided to learn how to ski and jumped into lessons in New York City on Saks Fifth Avenue's carpeted slide sprinkled with Borax. Outdoorsy and athletic, (at one time he was the #4 polo player in America), Harriman was a quick learner and soon became an excellent skier. (According to one story, Harriman skied so well that, on a diplomatic mission to Russia, he took time off for some runs and promptly left his bodyguard behind. After that, his security detail included a former member of Russia's ski team.) When the Count's wire arrived, Harriman was ready for his new endeavor and caught a train from New York City to Ketchum.

The moment he arrived, Harriman fell in love with the mountains and hills layered with snow against a brilliant blue sky. When Schaffgotsch took his boss to meet his new friends, the Brass family (whose descendants still live in the Valley), their ranch struck Harriman as the ideal site for the quiet, luxurious, vacation lodge he had in mind. And the timing was right: the Brass' had been struggling with recent cattle losses and, perhaps with a sigh of relief as well as sadness, they agreed to sell the family's well-placed, sunny 3,888 acres to Harriman for a bargain $39,000 (roughly $730,000 today).

With his purchase, Harriman opened the gates to the Wood River Valley's future. It probably took less than an hour for word to spread that a rich man had come to town to build a $1,000,000 ski resort in Ketchum. There would be lots of work for the next several months, starting NOW! Not that the Valley's economy was entirely moribund. The *Hailey Times* of 1936-1937 carried advertisements for local businesses, many of them offering new services that had sprung up across the nation: jewelers, insurers, beauty shops, dry cleaners, and J.C. Penney. For entertainment, one could enjoy The Kentucky Coon Hunters at the Oddfellows Hall or take in a film at the Liberty Theater.

Previously, the Valley had been dependent for its basic income on outside corporations eager to buy furs, ores, and sheep, as well as visitors who loved the hot springs. Now, in Harriman, the Valley had found someone with enough capital to build a big new enterprise that could, once again, generate economic prosperity. Their hopes were justified when Harriman hired lots of locals, 400 workers laid off from Idaho's Civilian Conservation Corps, and another 1,200 workers imported from California.

Pulling the Resort Team Together

The most important step completed – finding the perfect spot for his destination resort — Harriman returned to New York City to recruit the team that would design, build, market, and run it. He had always gravitated toward the most capable people and this was true of the team he chose to create his Resort.

It included Schaffgotsch, familiar with European resorts and the European style of hospitality; architect Gilbert Stanley Underwood, known for his 'rustic,' natural looking style that marked the hotels and rail stations he had built for Union Pacific's Utah Parks Commission;

Charlie Proctor, a member of the 1928 Olympic Team and a Harvard ski coach who could lay out runs and teach local boys the ways of the mountain; and Steve Hannigan, a flamboyant New York City publicist who, a decade earlier, had transformed Miami Beach from an attractive strip of sand into a famous playground for celebrities and socialites.

It would have been fun to watch these high-powered, temperamentally different men work together. Harriman was a persevering problem-solver who disdained social rules and wore rumpled clothes. He was aloof with most people unless they could help him turn his visions into reality. One friend nicknamed him "The Crocodile" because, overhearing a foolish comment in a meeting, Harriman, seeming to be asleep, would suddenly open his eyes and snap at the person like a crocodile.

Schaffgotsch was personally charming and knowledgeable about resort life, a charming young flirt who loved women. Proctor was an expert in ski terrain and a great ski coach. The outgoing Underwood had a national reputation and socialized easily in the higher echelons of Los Angeles. Hannigan loved flair, celebrity, and being in the sun with women, but hated winter and sports. In all things, though, drama was in his soul. Once, in a wire to the United Press from Miami Beach, Hannigan announced that millionaire Julius Fleischmann had "dropped dead on the polo field," adding "Don't forget Miami Beach Dateline!" A six-page *Life* magazine story, "Steve Hannigan's Girls," described him as "the man who, year in and year out, gets more pictures of [bathing girls] into the paper."[16]

Despite their differing personalities, the group apparently collaborated well, producing America's first destination ski resort in a seven-month window between May and December of 1936: a stunning and unique get-away in a timeless mountain valley where the hills were just right for novice skiers learning to stem christie before retiring to wine, dine, and sleep in luxurious style.

From the start, however, Hannigan had disdained Harriman's plan for a low-key, 100-room ski club for wealthy guests, with a few private homes built discretely nearby. In his world, a long-distance jaunt, especially to what he probably considered the god-forsaken State of Idaho, must culminate in a spectacular experience. A guest must be virtually swept away.

Harriman was persuaded and, when the Lodge opened a short few months later, it had 220 rooms, a beauty parlor, a barber shop, an elevator, a greenhouse for fresh cut flowers, a Saks Fifth Avenue branch with Sun Valley branded skiwear, a surgical center, a game room, and landscaping that included 1,500 newly planted trees. Rooms were finished in redwood and oak with copper fittings and furnished with thickly stuffed furniture upholstered in red or green. An outdoor dipping pool with warm water that overlooked snow-covered ridges was screened from the wind by tall glass walls. Ultimately, the hotel's construction cost Union Pacific $1,500,000 in 1936 dollars, three times the original estimate.

Although Harriman was personally a penny-pincher, he was confident that spending lots of pennies on the Resort would yield a solid return on investment. The United States was still working its way out of the Depression, but Harriman sensed the economy was heading upward toward a bright future. So, he indulged Hannigan's instincts and counted on reaping financial rewards in the long run.

Hannigan's campaign to market the Resort was intense and successful. He had convinced Harriman to change the name from "Ketchum Resort Hotel" to the more evocative "Sun Valley Lodge," and added the tagline, "Winter sports under a summer sun." He hit the print media hard, promoting the Resort as a glamourous get-away where adventure and romance flourished on every slope, behind each pine tree, and throughout the luxurious hotel. It was Miami in the mountains. Marketing included posters of young men and women dressed in colorful outdoor clothing and frolicking on sunny, snow-covered slopes, as well as bathing beauties lounging at the outdoor pool against the backdrop of sunny mountain tops tipped in white. One memorable poster portrayed a handsome, well-built, shirtless young man in black pants, casually standing on skis on a snow white hill as he wiped a mild sweat from his face. The photo was shot in a New York City studio, the sweat was Vaseline, and it was likely the young man had no idea how to ski!

When Hannigan announced that the Resort would open on the first day of winter, December 21, 1936, the media went full steam ahead. *Life* magazine ran an eight-page spread proclaiming, "East Goes West to Idaho's Sun Valley: Society's Newest Winter Playground" with photographs by Alfred Eisenstaedt, one of the magazine's most noted photographers.[17] Visitors were primed to anticipate a unique and memorable winter holiday in a setting that was brilliantly sunny, surprisingly warm, and terrifically self-indulgent.

Sun Valley Resort Opens

Harriman's winter Valhalla opened on time with great fanfare to three hundred expectant guests who arrived by train in Shoshone from around the country, likely having partied the whole way. From there they were bused to the Resort and greeted with a band, flowers and, perhaps, champagne. The invitees were drawn from Harriman's Park Avenue guest list and Junior League groups across the country (the League had been founded by Harriman's sister, Mary). It included state Governors, Hollywood directors and actors, and socialites from San Francisco, Boston, Chicago, Cincinnati, and Denver. A native Idahoan and columnist for The *New York Herald Tribune,* Inez Callaway Robb, proudly gushed that celebrities and socialites from both coasts were rushing to her home state to ski the beautiful Sawtooth Mountain slopes "with hickory bed slats strapped to their feet."[18]

There was just one problem that dimmed the opening's luster: The Valley had virtually no snow. When news spread beyond the Resort that barely a sprinkling of flakes (followed by rain) had left sagebrush shrubs jutting from the slopes, some guests sent their regrets. Harriman, determined to give the Resort a strong start, immediately directed that everyone could enjoy themselves free of charge until skiable snow appeared. For several days, guests enjoyed the hotel's outdoor ice rink, heated outdoor pool, dog sledding, bowling, bridge, and movies in the Opera House. They danced to band music in the Duchin room (named for Marie Duchin, pianist Eddie Duchin's wife, the room's designer, and a close friend of the Harrimans). They lingered over tasty meals concocted by French chefs and served by German waiters, experiencing a European aura in the middle of the mountain wilderness. For her grand entrance at dinner, a starlet could pose at the dining room's double doors and slowly descend the sweeping staircase in full view of other diners, surely a Hannigan brainstorm!

At last, on New Year's Eve, two feet of snow fell in the Valley. Now guests could enjoy two entirely new resort inventions. One was the first chairlift in the United States. Hannigan had laid the seed for the idea. During the Resort's construction, he had been horrified to learn that guests were expected to hike up a hill so they could ski down it. Although standard practice everywhere, Hannigan insisted that Sun Valley Resort guests be carried to the hilltop for their ski adventure. Harriman agreed and asked Union Pacific engineers to create a "chairlift." One of them, previously involved in developing loading equipment for bananas, mentally transformed a bunch of bananas into a human body and, with some tweaking, came up with what Hannigan wanted. From then on, skiers could sit a few feet above the ground on a chair hung from a moving cable and ride comfortably up a snowy hill. One chairlift each was installed on Proctor and Dollar mountains.

At the top of their downhill slide, skiers were introduced to Harriman's second invention: the ski school. Despite the sport's growing following, most people had no idea how to ski. It could be frightening and dangerous. Harriman solved the problem by dispatching Count Schaffgotsch to Austria to recruit six handsome ski instructors willing to emigrate to America to teach the sport. One of them, a charming alpine ski champion named Hans Hauser, became the ski school's Director and implemented popular "Learn to Ski" weeks. Guests were taught how to arc their way down a snow-covered hill on thin wooden slats, first using the snowplow and then advancing to parallel turns using the new European Arlberg technique. The school was a success but, lacking administrative skills and a play-boy to boot, Hauser was replaced after three seasons by Freidl Pfei-ffer, another excellent Austrian skier who expanded the Resort's ski school to 100 instructors.

In 1938, Harriman imported Pat "Pappy" Rogers from the Utah Parks Commission's North Rim Hotel at the Grand Canyon to run Sun Valley Resort. Pappy was a great choice. He hired wholesome young women and men who thrived in the warm family aura he cre-ated. On a summer's day, anyone near one of Pappy's beloved softball games might be ordered to join the fun and leave their work behind. A Ketchum resident who worked for Pappy as a young woman recalls: "He loved young people. There was hardly anyone whose name he did not remember. He was kind of a saint." After a snowfall (before the advent of groomers), Pappy could easily round up locals, instructors, and employees to jump on their skis and pack the runs.

Celebrities loved him too. When Ernest Hemingway and his third wife, Martha Gellhorn, visited the Resort in 1939, Pappy gave them discounted and often high-end room and board on and off for a couple of years. During that time, Hemingway edited the galleys of *For Whom the Bell Tolls*, his novel about the Spanish Civil War. Gellhorn, who loved peace and quiet when she was not reporting on a war some-where, praised Pappy's careful attention to guests. And she reveled in contemplating the "lion's skin" mountains backed by their "marvelous cool blond light" as "history whizzed by somewhere else."

Pappy's benevolent management style was in line with Harriman's belief that a business should do right by employees. The Resort paid well and provided good living conditions. In today's money, laborers received $18.10 per hour, carpenters $31.50 per hour, and college students $21.00 per hour. They and their families had free room and board in Union Pacific tents, shacks, and boxcars (modified for basic comfort), or else rented space from locals.

Harriman Expands the Resort

In its first year, Sun Valley Resort enjoyed 4,000 guests and Union Pacific's income from passenger tickets reached a high of $250,000 (about $4.7 million in today's dollars). While the figure did not cover the Resort's operating expenses, Harriman was confident he had created a social and recreational success that was worth a "small" investment by Union Pacific with its "great big income."

Still, Harriman ultimately wanted the Resort to pay for itself. In addition to attracting celebrities and the wealthy, he wanted it to be affordable for middle-class guests, ski racers, instructors, and other ski enthusiasts who "were not long in the pocketbook." In the Resort's second year, he built the more reasonably priced Challenger Inn, named for the railroad's remodeled line of trains. Each of the Inn's 200 rooms slept four people at $4 per night (bathroom down the hall) compared to the Lodge's single rooms for $10 per night (bathroom also down the hall).

The Inn's block-long facade was designed and painted to look like a row of small, colorful shops on a charming Tyrolean street facing a grassy green. It soon became the favored hang-out for ski instructors, employees, and easy-going celebrities who found the Lodge too formal. Ski racers from Europe and America thrived at the Inn as well, their expenses paid by Harriman when they visited to compete in the Harriman Cup, the Resort's first annual international race. Inaugurated in 1937, the Cup offered the biggest prize in American ski racing and ensured the Resort's international reputation as a ski destination.

Soon, the race became the climax of the winter season. "Will we see you at the Harriman Cup?" was the skiing equivalent of "Will we see you at the Kentucky Derby?"

That same year, Harriman installed other adventures for guests. The nation had a new interest in ski jumping, so he recruited Sigmund Ruud, one of the world's best jumpers, to construct a competitive jump site. Ruud chose a slope between Proctor and Dollar Mountains for a 15-meter ramp whose take-off table would thrust skiers into graceful airborne flight while people watched from below. Next, Harriman asked Florian Haemmerle to start an Alpine Touring School and followed it up with Pioneer Cabin built high in the nearby mountains for a touring destination. Finally, he added trails for cross-country skiing, still relatively new to America, and held the first race at Galena in 1939.

In the Resort's third year, Harriman and his team decided it was time to open Baldy's challenging terrain. Those eager to text their skills on steeper slopes were soon able to ski three runs accessed by a long chairlift that ultimately required three sections. Total rider capacity grew to about 450 per hour. By 1940, skiers from around the United States (including the Resort's next owner, Bill Janss) were training on Baldy for the upcoming Olympics. Then, Harriman made it possible for skiers to lunch on the mountain, building the Roundhouse restaurant, an octagonal building with a spectacular view that still reigns over its high mountain perch.

Nor were the delights of summertime overlooked. Mindful of those who loved hunting and fishing, Harriman purchased the beautiful Silver Creek Ranch, south of Hailey, and hired guides to squire people around. Other available sports included tennis, golf, skating on the outdoor ice rink, horseback riding, and hiking. Finally, visitors were encouraged to travel 60 miles north to Stanley to raft the famous Salmon River. In everything he did, Harriman thought in inclusive terms: working with the local community, reaching out to different socioeconomic groups, challenging adventurers to explore the wider region, and providing multiple recreation opportunities. Growing guest numbers was important to him, but the richness of a guest's experience was even more so.

The Resort's reputation and the Valley's prestige grew, particularly after 1941 when Darryl F. Zanuck, 20th Century Fox's studio chief, produced the movie *Sun Valley Serenade* at the Resort. The film's plot unveiled a three-way love triangle between a band's pianist, the band's singer, and a female ice skater. The set was the rustic, yet luxurious, Sun Valley Lodge perched among sunny, snow-covered hills dotted with ski runs edged by stately fir trees. Zanuck loved the resort and chose it to showcase Norwegian Olympic figure skater Sonia Henie, a Fox box office winner. Making the film in the Resort's relative isolation cost Fox an extravagant $1.3 million (about $24 million today), even with Henie's scenes filmed in a Hollywood studio, but the location was ideal for Zanuck to pursue his real-life three-way love triangle with his French girlfriend.

Sun Valley Serenade enchanted moviegoers across the United States, its success likely tempting Hannigan to do backflips, if he could, to celebrate the ensuing publicity. Sun Valley was now on the nation's map as a place to visit and, increasingly, a place to be seen.

The War and Post-War Years

When America joined World War II on December 7, 1941, Sun Valley Resort's operations were temporarily diverted. At Harriman's request, it became a Naval Convalescent Hospital with 1,600 beds for veterans suffering from physical wounds and combat fatigue. Sheltered in the serene mountain environment, the hospital's male and female patients enjoyed "rest, good diet, psychotherapy, or physiotherapy," plus educational programs to prepare them for re-entering civilian life. For some rowdier patients, the hospital's isolation and restricted liberty were frustrating, but others enjoyed the indoor and outdoor recreation in a restful place.[19]

When the war ended in September 1945, the Resort took more than a year to refurbish itself, reopening in December 1946. Most of the pre-war staff was gone. Freidl Pfeiffer and Hans Hauser had been investigated in 1942 as possible German spies and, although cleared of charges, they were given just two options. Pfeiffer chose to fight on the Italian front in the 10th Mountain Division with other Wood River Valley ace skiers; Hauser elected detention in North Dakota. Both returned to the Valley briefly after the war, but Pfeiffer soon moved to Aspen to help build its fame and fortune, taking several instructors and celebrity clients with him.

A more desperate Hauser eloped with his sweetheart, Virginia Hill, a Mafia money courier and Resort guest. Their lives were troubled, and both reportedly died of suicide at separate times. Schaffgotsch never had the chance to return, not that Harriman would have let him; he proved to be a Nazi and fought and died for Hitler. Underwood moved to Washington. D.C. Only Otto Lang returned to run the ski school before leaving in 1950 to pursue a filmmaking career begun in Sun Valley.

Prior to the war, Sun Valley Resort had enjoyed what might be viewed as its childhood and adolescence as a freewheeling enclave where Resort guests and Ketchum locals intermingled easily to gamble, drink, and party into the night. The wealthy hung out with the ski bum, the socialite with the instructor, and the starlet with the bartender in an atmosphere of adventure, health, escape, and privilege. Johnny Lister, whose trio played at the Lodge, praised the Resort for its egalitarian atmosphere where "you could find yourself skiing with a dish washer or an MIT Ph.D."

After the war, the Resort became more polished in its operations, much of it due to Dorice Taylor. She and her husband, two of the Resort's first guests, had fallen in love with the place and, when the Resort reopened in 1946, Hannigan hired Taylor to run public relations. She was great at marketing to people with discretionary income for leisure and recreation: business moguls, actors, politicians, society matrons, millionaire playboys, and heads of state. But she was also able to attract business conventions and the emerging middle-class, many of whom were veterans aided by the G.I. Bill.

Clever, creative, and attuned to what appealed to vacationers, Taylor was a major boon to the Resort, marketing the possibilities of skiing in the Boulder mountains on a spring morning and playing golf at the Resort in the afternoon. Her book, *Sun Valley*, tells wonderful tales.[20] Once, when the Resort was closed for the season, she satisfied Groucho Marx's request to marry his sweetheart in a scant two hours, producing a minister, wedding cake, champagne, and flowers. And she secured the filming of "Bus Stop," starring Marilyn Monroe, at the Valley's North Fork store above Ketchum. Above all, it was Taylor's exceptional customer service and publicity efforts that reawakened post-war interest in the Resort. Some say she put Idaho on the map. In her *New York Herald Tribune* column, Inez Robb wrote that Taylor made the nation more aware of Idaho than "all her chambers of commerce" could ever hope to do.

While Taylor revived the Resort's reputation, the Wood River Valley resumed much of its lively lifestyle of pre-war years. The Pioneer Restaurant, built in 1940 for gambling (not permitted at the Resort), once again had cowboys and celebrities betting and socializing together. One of the best-liked men in town was the Sheriff, "Lester the Arrester." And people forgave the often-inebriated fire chief who was said to cause more water damage at fires than the flames themselves. Local bands filled saloons with loud music, including the hokey pokey ("put your right foot in and put your right foot out"), the most popular dance in town.

Many of the locals were ski bums caught up in the Valley's delights. Ready to feed on peanut butter sandwiches and drink Pabst

Blue Ribbon, they crammed in with friends at Lefty's Cabins, Antlers Hotel, or Tequila Flats, "willing to be stacked like cordwood" for the chance to ski Sun Valley. Others camped year-round in the Valley's woods, hanging out at the local saloons until just before bedtime. Warren Miller, hired as a ski instructor, began his filmmaking career in 1947, shooting the first ski documentaries while living in a teardrop camper in River Run's parking lot and supposedly hunting dinner outside his front door.

Eventually, a good number of ski bums settled down to start families and, wanting a more reliable income, they opened businesses, grew the community's economy, and formed close social ties. Sturtevant's of Sun Valley, the oldest retail ski store in the United States, opened in 1948 to sell athletic clothing and equipment. Families shopped at the Golden Rule department store (an Idaho chain at the time) or grabbed a bite at the Western Café, which lasted 50 years until it closed in 2004. Still going strong today, after seven decades of growing along with the Valley, are Atkinson's Market (1956) and Michels' Christiana Restaurant (1959).

The Resort Drops to Second Place

Even as the Valley grew, however, major change was sneaking in the back door. Harriman, despite loving his Resort for its "old-fashioned comfort and graciousness," had realized that Washington, D.C. was replacing Wall Street as the axis of power. A man who enjoyed living at the center of events, he turned his career toward public affairs and government service. In 1941, he became President Roosevelt's envoy to Europe, managing the lend-lease arrangement that allowed the United States to sell military equipment to Britain and other countries for their defense in World War II. He served as Ambassador to the Soviet Union (1943-1946) and was Secretary of Commerce under President Truman (1946-1948). As his post-War presence at "Averell's hotel in Idaho" (as Omaha headquarters called it) diminished, the Resort's spirit and cachet inevitably dimmed, as well as Union Pacific's corporate commitment.

At the same time, the Resort began to face serious competition. Having introduced the destination resort, chairlift, and ski school, vastly enhancing a skier's experience, Harriman's prediction of a new industry for the Mountain West was fulfilled. Other mountain towns adopted his ideas and built their own destination ski areas, reducing Harriman's early competitive advantage. Aspen opened to the public in 1946 and quickly shot toward the apex of ski resorts. Other ski areas sprouted in Western states and attracted their own set of celebrities and ski afficionados. The competition for accolades and visitors hit the Resort and the Valley hard, perhaps explaining the population decline from 5,384 residents in 1950 to 4,598 in 1960.

By the mid-1950s, Union Pacific's president, Arthur Stoddard, was closely watching his bottom line. Rail travel was declining in favor of cars, planes, and buses. In addition, the Resort had cost Union Pacific $500,000-$1,000,000 per year for several years ($5.5-$10.5 million today). For Stoddard, Harriman's beloved Idaho enclave was a distant, relentlessly costly, and unwanted outlier to the core business. When Pappy Rogers was told to stop providing cut flowers to guests in 1952, he saw the writing on the wall and returned to the Utah Parks Commission. Union Pacific replaced him with an economizing Winston McCrea who cut back on every possible expense. In 1953, Steve Hannigan died. Dorice Taylor took his place and stayed at the Resort until 1971, but the Resort's spirit was waning. When the Harriman Cup was cancelled that year, its reputation among the ski elite dimmed. In Jack Hemingway's words, Harriman's absence from the Resort had ultimately put it in "far more prosaic and less imaginative hands."

The Resort slid downhill over the next decade. That Omaha headquarters was indifferent to the place had become more and more apparent. Infrastructure was deteriorating; buildings needed remodeling, and locals began to lift china, furniture, and other items from the premises. One man wrote to Harriman about the deep and increasing discontent, saying, 'Gone is the warm, friendly atmosphere of bygone years. More and more old-time guests have got fed up and do not come back." Without Harriman's aura, inspirational energy, and visible commitment to the Resort, its initial "glory days" were ending.

In Retrospect

It is likely that only a person with Harriman's vision, leadership, wealth, business experience, creative thinking, and social influence could have built Sun Valley Resort and its national reputation in such a short period of time.[21] Owning a railroad that could fund the Resort and provide transportation for its guests gave him a significant advantage, and for that he was always grateful, openly acknowledging that his wealth gave him the security to freely pursue his goals. Shaped by the noblesse oblige tradition of his time, Harriman was egalitarian and generous. His values helped create the Resort's culture, and percolated into the community as a leader's values usually do, founding the unpretentious atmosphere that has lasted, for the most part, ever since.

Visiting Sun Valley Resort in his 80s, Harriman shared his great regret that his beloved "hotel in Idaho" had been sold by Union Pacific years earlier. He was 45 years old when he built the Resort and 73 years old when it was sold. All that time he had loved it, but gradually, and willingly, he had relinquished influence over its direction. As a businessman, he could understand that the Resort had become a white elephant for Union Pacific. It was far from Omaha headquarters, unrelated to Union Pacific's interests, and hemorrhaging money; he knew the railroad must come to terms with its problematic orphan child. But he could proud that he had inaugurated a new industry and provided a solid economic foothold for the Valley as it headed into the future.

Chapter Three[22]

Benevolent Ski Enthusiast: Bill Janss

"It would be a slam-dunk to make this mountain."

— Bill Janss

Enter Bill and Ed Janss, the third generation of the Janss Investment Company, a successful real estate development operation in Southern California founded in 1884 by their grandfather, Dr. Peter Janss. A Danish immigrant, Dr. Janss had taken his medical training in Iowa but decided to open his practice in Los Angeles which, with its newly discovered oil deposits and direct railroad access, was becoming one of the most dynamic economic regions in America.

Before long, the ambitious doctor realized that land development would be even more lucrative than medicine. With his two young sons, Harold and Edwin, he founded the Janss Investment Company and, over the next three decades, the Company developed a host of residential communities throughout the Los Angeles area. Yorba Linda, Holmby Hills, Van Nuys, and Monterey Park were just part of the roughly 90,000 acres of prime Southern California property that the *Los Angeles Times* dubbed "the Janss Dynasty."[23]

Dr. Janss' son, Harold, married well and, in 1922, his father-in-law gifted him a scenic 3,300-acre parcel near Los Angeles which he and his brother developed into Westwood Village. It was the first "urban core" development in the United States with commercial properties surrounded by residential areas. It was stunning — 1,000 homes and businesses designed with clay tiled roofs, Spanish wall tiles, and outdoor patios in the Mediterranean style — and praised for having the best planned layout in the country. As the Village was being developed, the Janss' connected with the growing University of California and suggested it might expand into Westwood, offering a $3 million parcel to the University for $1 million. The win-win deal greatly assisted the University and helped guarantee Westwood's ultimate success as a community.

The Third Janss Generation

By the mid-1940s, Dr. Janss' grandchildren, brothers Ed and Bill, had taken over the Janss Investment Company. Ed was the chairman, strategic thinker, financial manager, and a well-regarded collector of fine art and thoroughbred racehorses. Bill was entrepreneurial, visionary, and outgoing, and an environmentalist before the term was popular. Both were liberal and community oriented. (Years later, Ed made Nixon's "enemies list" when he protested the Vietnam War.)[24]

More than anything, though, brother Bill adored skiing. When he was six, he fell in love with the sport on a family vacation at the famed Ahwahnee Hotel in Yosemite Valley (designed by Gilbert Underwood, the architect for Sun Valley Resort) and honed his skills every vacation thereafter. In college at Stanford, Bill studied industrial engineering, but skiing always topped his agenda. He created the University's first ski team and, by 1940, was himself a contender for that year's Olympics, training one winter on Baldy and racing in the Harriman Cup.

(Unfortunately, the Olympics were cancelled due to World War II). After serving in the war as a pilot, Bill briefly ran Yosemite's winter sports program but then decided to join his family's real estate firm.

During a slowdown in the California real estate market, Bill rode the range to manage the family's cattle operations. In the process, his entrepreneurial drive took hold. "We own(ed) farmland and cattle and we say, very naively, 'Well, why don't we feed our own animals?'"[25] He and his brother bought a feedlot in Thermal, California where Bill built state-of-the-art grain mills that produced an innovative corn-flake-like feed. In his words, "Cattle feeding was fairly new, and the old-timers were kind of like old...We were the second generation of cattle people and we just...had a lot of fun because we related more to the colleges, the universities where the latest techniques were being developed."

Next, Janss organized a research center with other ranchers to explore new approaches to managing cattle. Among his peers, he was the first to use hormones to raise animal weight per pound of feed. "It was an exciting period," according to Janss. At the peak of his efforts, he was responsible for feeding roughly 50,000 head of cattle for various clients which was "maybe not quite as exciting as running Sun Valley but we were doing the finest job in the world at that moment."

In 1952, Janss was ready to buy a second home in ski country and followed his buddies to Aspen, the new star in the growing firmament of destination ski resorts. The Aspen Ski Company recruited him to its board, but he soon found the role frustrating. Anticipating major growth in the ski industry, he pressed the Company to expand Aspen's ski terrain, but was unsuccessful and finally resigned, having decided that the board was "not very savvy about the ski business."

Bill's brother and other friends agreed with his sense of the future, however. In 1958, they began quietly buying ranches in the Brush Creek area, just five miles from Aspen, where they planned to build a European-styled resort. Janss would jump into his Cessna to survey possible purchases, just as his dad had done with him in California decades earlier. Eventually, when the group had acquired enough property, they named the area "Snowmass" and announced that Snowmass Resort would open in 1967-1968.

In 1963, while they were working on Snowmass, Union Pacific's President, Arthur Stoddard, hired the Janss' to create a plan to resurrect Sun Valley Resort, the railroad's white elephant. After taking a close look in 1963, the brothers recommended injecting $5,000,000 to bring the facilities up to snuff, as well as extensive residential and commercial development. For Stoddard, the plan was the nail in the Resort's coffin. He had always scorned residential development, saying he was not going to build homes for people who would spend their money in Ketchum. Nor had Omaha ever looked kindly on the enterprise. With Harriman deeply engaged in other interests, Stoddard decided to end the railroad's decades-long losses. It was time for Union Pacific — and the Resort — to go their separate ways.

Taking on Sun Valley Resort

Since the Janss brothers had identified how to reinvigorate Sun Valley Resort, Stoddard asked if they might be interested in buying it. They were — and they did — for a scant $3 million, planning to invest another $30 million to turn it into the dream get-away that Bill envisioned. The entire Resort had cost the railroad nearly $5,000,000 to build under Harriman, but at that point was valued at only about $750,000 and was a money pit. In later comments on the transaction, Stoddard noted how incongruous it had been for Union Pacific to own a resort and how glad he was that the new owners would know best how to take care of it.

Buying Sun Valley Resort was a big commitment for the Janss brothers, considering their involvement with Snowmass. Further, they bought the Resort in November 1964, just one month before its Christmas opening. For the 46-year-old Bill, however, there was no hesitation. "Well, good gosh," he said later. "You only get the chance to buy a national park once....it was the opportunity of a lifetime." The timing seemed especially good since Janss sensed that the ski industry was about to surge. Owning the federal government's lease to operate Baldy, he could take what he said was "the best ski mountain in the world" to even greater heights. A couple of thousand miles away, Omaha headquarters' relief at finally shedding its nearly 30-year-old odd stepchild was probably the cause for long-awaited celebration.

Janss had his work cut out for him as the Resort's renovator and land developer. The financial records, to the extent they existed, were messy. Union Pacific had absorbed the costs of core items such as food and fuel, commingling the Resort's accounts with its own. Expenses could only be guessed for everything from wages to utilities and maintenance to publicity. The Resort also had 17 unions, coordinated by the Sun Valley Trades Council, whose involvement Bill didn't particularly like, saying they were "Nice old boys but...spoiled because Union Pacific would settle any problem with them. They didn't want it to get out to be a national issue."

Janss realized he needed someone to help him manage the Resort's operations. He was a champion skier and great at land development and cattle feeding, but running a resort was another thing entirely. He found management frustrating. One staffer recalls, "He was an owner who cared about the mission statement but...didn't understand bottom-up budgeting." Another explained, "He could be impossible to work for...away a lot and unpredictable, frequently changing his mind. He'd come to meetings with new, far-out ideas and miss the fact that the retail stores were struggling." According to Dorice Taylor, who was still working in publicity, he sent her lots of memos which she would pile on her desk. Then, she would show them to him and ask, "Do you really want me to do this?" to which, she reports, he rarely answered "Yes."

Janss wisely hired Harry Holmes in 1965, an accomplished hotel and resort manager he had met at Snowmass. Within two years, Holmes was Resort President and CEO, directing the many additions and improvements called for by Janss. He was good on the administrative side as well, introducing computers, up-to-date accounting practices, and a management training program for talented employees.

The Resort's restoration began in earnest to achieve Janss' vision of a relaxed year-round retreat where middle-class guests could indulge in comfort, fun, and elegance at a decent price. Like Harriman, he wanted to provide families that lacked the time and money to visit European resorts with a taste of them in Idaho. Yet, he also wanted to maintain the quality that attracted celebrities like Jackie Kennedy and her children in 1966.

The Lodge rooms were upgraded and the Challenger Inn's dormitory-style, bathroom-down-the-hall rooms renovated into more appealing en suite singles. At the heart of the Resort, in the open space between the Lodge and the Inn, Janss expanded the quaint European-style village with eateries, a grassy square, tennis courts, a creek, a pond, and retail shops that sold the first Head skis and Bogner ski pants in the United States. Cars were forbidden and the quiet, pedestrian-only space offered a peaceful place to meander. Looking around the Resort's basement, deserted after its coal heat had been replaced with less expensive natural gas, Janss imagined what soon became the Boiler Room, the Resort's high spot for many years of late-night entertainment. Finally, he hired Peter Schott, inventor of the New American Cuisine, to be the Resort's head chef.

But the Lodge, Inn, and Boiler Room would be nothing without guests. In Harriman's time, visitors typically arrived via Union Pacific's Oregon Short Line. Just before the Janss brothers bought the Resort, however, the railroad had terminated service at Shoshone, leaving Ketchum high and dry. Janss solved the problem by arranging non-stop flights from Los Angeles and San Francisco to Twin Falls.

There, visitors could catch his new Snow Valley Company buses to Sun Valley, resting or sightseeing along the way.

Janss' easy-going style worked well in a community of urban escapees, many of them ski bums who were serious about having fun. It was the 1960s after all and "The Valley was home to hippies, small service and retail shops, Basques, and ranchers," according to one local septuagenarian. After Harriman's long absence and Union Pacific's indifference to the Resort, Bill stepped into a yawning gap for an enthusiastic owner. Living in Ketchum, he was visible and approachable, someone who readily interacted with people in a welcoming manner. (Meeting a new person, Janss reportedly would grab the person's hand, and declare, "Great to meet you. Where you from?") He hired locals — too many according to some — and, although he gave them scant pay, he provided lots of perks: free room and board, a ski jacket and hat, and a free ski pass. One retired local who had been a waiter at the Boiler Room three nights a week said the free ski pass was one of his most precious possessions.

Soon, Janss developed a loyal following that paid off in unexpected ways. Early in his ownership, for example, a strike by the United Airlines and Mechanics Union shut down the chairlifts; as word spread, locals volunteered to run the lifts and fill other operational roles until the strike ended. "We were like a club then," says one old-timer.

Bill's Solo Turn with the Resort

Just two years after the Janss brothers bought Sun Valley Resort, they began to develop Snowmass in partnership with the Aspen Ski Company. Aspen was to build the ski operations while brother Bill designed the village at the Resort's base. There he planned an on-mountain Zermatt-style pedestrian-only settlement ("cars are intrusive") with ski-in/ski-out homes clustered in the hills and connected by trails. Unfortunately, conflict arose between Bill and Aspen's building contractor, American Cement, when it overruled his design to unite the mountain and the village. At that point, he said, "with the mountain separated from the village…that was the end of it for me as far as fun. It was the city against the mountain…the people."

When Snowmass opened in 1967, the Janss brothers promptly sold their shares back to Aspen Ski Company. (Bill could be proud, however, that his initial instincts to inaugurate a second resort at Aspen were spot-on: Snowmass opened to 100,000 skier visits in its first season, the most for any new destination resort at the time.) At that point, flush with cash, Bill proposed to buy Ed's shares in Sun Valley Resort and to sell Ed his shares in the family's real estate business. Perhaps he wanted to work more independently or simply get out of real estate per se. He was, after all, a skier deep at heart. In an interview, he confessed that neither he nor his brother enjoyed selling real estate, saying, "I've always kind of disliked it…real estate salesmen…trying to sell you something as high as they can." At any rate, the brothers made a deal.

Bill was now the sole owner of Sun Valley Resort. Working with Harry Holmes, he was responsible for the Resort's physical plant (two hotels, open land, and all recreational facilities), staff management, guest amenities, marketing, finances, national reputation, growth, and future success, using his own dime, brains, and bank loans. Above all, he was responsible for residential development. In 1965, Janss had gained approval from the Idaho Legislature to build and sell condominiums, a type of residence approved in other states, but not yet in Idaho. This approach enabled Janss to retain all condo sales rights, bypass sales agents, and maintain tight control over the pricing and pace of residential growth, avoiding what he called "the willy-nilly construction" happening in Aspen and Vail.

As he began to build condos near the Resort's Inn and Lodge, his friendly manner probably helped counterbalance local dismay about the construction; people complained about the Company's encroachment onto space once open to horseback riding, hunting, and meandering. But the Valley's builders, their employees, and the overall economy were benefitting. Other good news was that the Janss Investment Company had always been committed to preserving open space, rather than building man-made structures everywhere. During three generations of development in California and Hawaii, the Janss' had protected as much natural beauty, scenic vistas, and local wildlife terrain as possible. Just a few years before the company closed its doors in 1995, the University of Southern California's School of Architecture awarded the Janss Investment Company the "Parkinson Spirit of Urbanism Award," honoring 100 years of innovative land development dedicated to preserving a community's connection to nature.[26]

In the end, the condominium clusters rode the land's natural contours and were mostly hidden by landscaping. The earliest units were relatively luxurious compared to prefabricated units that came later, but, whether tiny, affordable studio "cottages" or larger homes, all continued to sell. For several years, the profits from one condominium's sales helped pay for the construction of the next. At one point, perhaps when Janss was short on money, he built condominiums with a barracks-like appearance that earned the nickname "Camp Janss." Even Janss called them "cookie cutter houses," but he relied on landscaping to improve their appearance.

Roughly 650-700 condominium units were built during Janss' tenure. With many of the new homes in the affordable category, younger people were able to get a foothold in the Valley for the first time. Janss also began to court second homeowners as buyers, a strategy that was eventually adopted by other ski resorts and dramatically changed the industry's face.[27] Looking back on constructing 60-70 units per year, what Janss called "no more than a little Austrian town," he said, "I was always afraid of making mistakes and creating problems. If you grow slowly, you see your needs and you build for those needs. We're not sprawled out all over the community."

Janss Turns to His Beloved Baldy

By 1967, Janss could finally devote himself to shaping his dream mountain. Condominium construction and sales were underway, he had access to bank loans, and he had cash from selling his shares in the Janss Investment Company. When first seeing Baldy many years earlier, he had said, "It would be a slam dunk to make this mountain." Now he could design the skier's paradise that lived in his dreams.

The mountain offered a rare, continuous 3,400-foot drop from a 9,150-foot summit. Its terrain was wonderfully varied: wide open spaces and views, generous bowls, thick surrounding forests, and both steep and not-so-steep flowing inclines. Janss was determined to cut runs for every skier level so no one would ever feel stuck or at risk for colliding with other skiers moving at faster or slower speeds. He wanted to create a ski experience that would be perfect for everyone: young kids, beginning adult skiers, and racing champions. This meant providing varying degrees of difficulty, as well as lifts that spread people across the mountain to eliminate long lines.

During the next decade, Janss expanded the number of Baldy's runs from 33 to 62, the number of chairlifts to 16, and expanded the mountain's per hour capacity from roughly 1,000 to 14,000 skiers. A signature achievement was opening Baldy's West side. Lurking there was Warm Springs, the longest, most cherished, downhill slide. Unfortunately, it ended just above a strip of private land owned by two sisters. Everyone loved the run but skied it only on the way home, stopping just before the sisters' property to take the bus back to town. As perhaps only he could, Janss persuaded the sisters to sell him the strip and soon skiers were free to cruise (or race) to the very bottom of Warm Springs before riding the chairlift back up on new cushioned seats, enfolded in warm capes. For many years, Warm Springs was the most heavily used base at the mountain. Skiers would arrive at 8:30 a.m., put their skis in line, and head to the lodge for a warm beverage before the lifts opened at 9:00 a.m.

Having created the still revered Warm Springs run, Janss could proudly and rightfully claim that Baldy was a mountain with the greatest ski terrain in the United States. A 2018 article in *Men's Journal* proclaimed, "The Warm Springs ski run on Baldy...is considered by many to be the best stretch of downhill in the country. The two-mile-long, top-to-bottom screamer charges straight through a natural gully with banked sidewalls before opening to the width of a California freeway. It never wavers from the fall line and maintains an average pitch of 35 degrees, without a single blind turn to slow you down."[28]

Janss' improvements to Baldy included creating a lively mountain atmosphere with friendly "ambassadors" skiing in elfin green outfits. Instructors had contracts that guaranteed set hours, commissions, and free room and board. One of them with over four decades on the mountain recalls: "It was an absolute blast, a great time for young people with tons of students coming through each week." Skiers of any age and ability could also compete in the on-mountain races that Harriman had started: the RAM, Silver Sun, Golden Sun, and Diamond Sun. Meanwhile, the ski school maintained its international reputation under the experienced leadership of Sigi Engl, hired as an instructor under Harriman in 1952 for his well-known and innovative alpine instruction methods.

A lot of thought, emotion and sweat equity went into Janss' turning Baldy into an outstanding ski experience for all comers. It was his passion. A stepson remembers that Janss liked to ski alone: "The lift line for single skiers was his choice so he could pump each rider for information: 'What do you like? Has anything changed for better or for worse since you were last here? What three things would you change if you could?'" This, his stepdad had said, was the only reliable way to find out what improvements were needed on Baldy. In the evening, he would ponder priorities: Was it more important to cut a run or add condos? Should he flush cut stumps or completely tear them out for smoother runs? His stepson once heard the front door close in the middle of the night; the next day he learned that Janss had gone to Baldy to help mountain crews finish-rake a marginally snowy slope.

Although Janss focused primarily on improving Baldy, he knew the value of providing other winter activities for guests. After heli-skiing in Canada in 1966, he started the first heli-ski operation in the United States in the Wood River Valley. Now, free-heel backcountry skiers hankering for powder could access thousands of acres of "cold smoke" slopes in local mountain ranges. Four years later, Janss worked with alpine instructor Leif Odmark, a Swedish Nordic and ski-jumping champion, to open the first Nordic Ski School and Touring Center in America with rental huts in the woods for ski-in-ski-out overnights. In 1974, he reinstated the World Cup on Baldy, reviving its reputation as a skiing mecca and, in 1975, he worked with Olympian ice skater Herman Maricich to build an indoor ice rink and start an ice hockey program.

That Damn Hospitality Business

If skiing was Janss' passion, running a business was a thorn in his side. He simply did not enjoy management and, at times, confided to select friends, "I love to ski but I hate this hotel business." Often, he stretched the patience of his staff with his empathy for young skiers; he called them "brown baggers" and opened a couple dozen free rides each morning on Baldy's lift if they could pack the steep spots that groomers couldn't navigate. For their work, they might earn a full-day lift ticket and an occasional free meal. "If they were lucky," wrote *Sun Valley* magazine, "brown baggers got the chance to sweep the mountain with the ski patrol after the lifts closed. What a score—skiing at the famous Sun Valley for free and hanging out with the beautiful people at night." On the other hand, there were those in the Resort's management ranks who called brown-baggers "free-loaders," and felt Janss kept too many people on the payroll, including slackers.

48

Ultimately, Janss' free-wheeling style frustrated Holmes, especially when Janss second-guessed his CEO's decisions and criticized a marketing strategy that relied more on word-of-mouth than direct spending. In return, Holmes objected to Janss' free hand with money when he was so carefully trying to manage the budget. In 1972, Holmes resigned to become president of Del Monte Properties, owner of Pebble Beach. By that time, however, he had helped Janss fulfill much of his vision while keeping the Resort in the black. He once proudly claimed that, under his hand, the Resort's operations enjoyed annual profits after 30 years of deficits under Union Pacific.[29]

Staying in the black did not last long, however. The year Holmes left, Janss sold 1,900 acres of the Resort's Elkhorn property for $300,000 to the Johns-Manville Corporation for development. Johns-Manville spent $7.9 million over the next few years building residences, shops, and cafes, while partnering with the Resort as its sales office. One early reviewer praised the development, saying, "The Wizard of Oz Would Love This Skiing Village."[30] In 1982, however, Johns-Manville incurred massive lawsuits for injuries from its asbestos-related products and filed for bankruptcy. After a brief period of lively restaurants and rock band performances under owner Milt Kuolt in the 1990s, Elkhorn fell into a kind of limbo with rarely occupied second-homes, a deserted atmosphere, and four more corporate owners.[31]

The man Janss picked to replace Holmes was not as good at budgeting, or managing his boss as Holmes had been; as the Resort's development continued, it began edging toward insolvency. In 1976, Janss opened Seattle Ridge terrain. Then, he spent $1 million (about $4.5 million today) to install snowmaking, an infant technology, on Baldy. Although one of the largest installations in the United States at the time, the machine-made snow covered just 40 acres of the mountain, too limited an area to make much difference. Janss also bought powerful and costly grooming machines that could knock down moguls carved by Baldy's skiers on its steeper slopes. Proud of the purchase, he said, "Turning on steeper slopes, the constant challenge of placing your turn...that's really what it's all about. Today I think we are really doing the finest job in grooming." Finally, Janss began to build Lookout, the Resort's first top-of-the-mountain lodge, and the Mayday lift to carry skiers straight to Baldy's magnificent bowls. The last two projects remained unfinished, however, as Janss finally came to terms with his financial problems.

Three successive events threw Janss off his perilous path. In the fall of 1973, the United States saw the start of the longest and deepest economic recession since World War II. The economy hit bottom in midwinter 1975 and threw the ski industry on its ear, just after Janss had invested in snowmaking and grooming. He also faced a $32 million lawsuit that had stalled major improvements to the Resort's Village. Finally, a 1976-1977 drought marked the ski season with a "new absolute minimum snow depth." It was the last blow. Just 80,000 skiers bought ski passes that winter and most mid-level managers were laid off at Christmas. Going into the spring, skiable snow ended halfway up the mountain and Baldy saw a scant 400-450 skiers per day riding the only two available lifts. What was left of Janss' reserve funds dried up and bank loans were denied. He had to face a harsh reality.

The End of an Era

In the winter of 1977, the 59-year-old Janss put Sun Valley Resort up for sale. He had exuberantly put his heart into reviving it as a fun family resort with a taste of Europe and a variety of winter recreation options. He had expanded Baldy's infrastructure, added ski runs, enlarged the mountain's carrying capacity, and organized transportation to bring visitors to the isolated Wood River Valley. He had put the Resort back on the map as a desirable place to visit, one with an incredible ski mountain in a down-to-earth, yet increasingly sophisticated, community. He was beloved by locals for his personality, generosity, and spirit. But he was tired, had experienced one heart attack, and was struggling with a cancer diagnosis. The strain of running the resort was huge. "It's like running 20 businesses at one time," he once said. "The economics are very bad. I do a heck of a lot better with my stock portfolio than running a resort." It was time to let go.

Shortly after Janss put the Resort on the market, the Walt Disney Company showed interest. At first a deal looked possible, but the entertainment behemoth pulled out after just a few weeks. Publicly, Disney said the Resort was not right for the year-round recreation concept it had in mind. Several locals believed Disney pulled out because of the pending lawsuit over the Resort Village. (Others thought it was because a visiting executive broke his leg skiing.) While Disney's withdrawal must have disappointed Janss, locals who feared a Disney-style Park were relieved. One businessman wrote to the *Idaho Mountain Express* that he had visited Florida's Disney World and found it a "dazzling, utterly stupendous amusement center" but he pleaded with the corporation, "Please don't do it to us."

Janss' next inquiry came from Earl Holding, a Salt Lake City oil and hotel magnate. His wife, Carol, had seen an article in *The Wall Street Journal* about the Resort's sale. The couple came, saw, and bought in a relatively quick, secret deal completed in April 1977. Janss would sell Sun Valley Resort to Holding for $12 million, $9 million more than he had originally paid. He also agreed to fire his entire work force of 1,400 employees so Holding could build his own operating team without worrying about union demands, something Janss understood. Nevertheless, it must have been hard for the friendly man who, in previous years, laid people off at the end of every season but knew he could hire them back in a few months.

Reflecting on his years owning the Resort, Janss said it had been lots of fun but he had always felt challenged financially, operationally, and personally. He had accomplished much of what he wanted for his Resort, but acknowledged "a kind of sameness after 12 or 13 years or so." In fact, Janss said he was happy that Holding's wealth would enable him to do even more with the Resort than he had been able to do. When all was said and done, Janss' spirit was at last free of the hospitality business, and people said he was more like his old self: happy, enthusiastic, and skiing just for the fun of it every day he could.

The Janss Legacy

Once out of the Resort business, Janss hopefully reflected on all he had done to enrich the Valley community. Most obviously, he had improved the Resort's facilities, created the country's best ski mountain, and introduced a host of new winter activities. He had also invested time and money in the Valley's overall quality of life, believing, as Harriman had, that a business should partner with its community to ensure mutual strength. His second wife, Glenn Janss, once described his idea of a healthy community as a place where all "human needs were met, not only spiritually and physically, but the more ethereal, creative and artistic sides."

One of his early efforts, along with his first wife, Anne, was to develop a local arts scene to enrich the Valley. To that end, they invited their friend, arts advocate Glenn Cooper, 1965 Los Angeles Woman of the Year, to move to Ketchum and become the arts advocate for the Valley.[32] Cooper, an energetic widow with five children, visited the Valley in 1968 and liked it. She agreed to move but was initially reluctant to lead the development of a local arts scene. One day, Janss took Cooper to a dog pound surrounded by seven lovely acres up Trail Creek (where the Community School now sits) and offered to remodel it as a center for the applied arts. It was an attractive prospect for Cooper and, once assured she could do it on her own terms, she founded the Sun Valley Creative Art Workshops for fine arts, ceramics, photography, and graphics.

Sadly, Anne Janss died in 1973 in an avalanche on Balcom Ridge (near Sun Valley) while heli-skiing. Janss and Cooper married and continued to partner in their avid support of the arts. The Sun Valley

Creative Art Workshops grew steadily, drawing artists and their colleagues to the Valley where they opened fine arts galleries, formed dance and theater companies, and produced rock, classical, and folk concerts.[33] Today, Glenn Janss' non-profit, renamed the Sun Valley Museum of Art, is the oldest arts organization in the Valley, mounting over 60 arts and humanities events each year with earnings of nearly $3,000,000.[34]

Janss' legacy includes two other efforts that significantly enhanced the Valley's quality of life. The first is the nationally known fishing gem, Silver Creek Preserve.[35] Harriman had bought the high desert, spring-fed 479-acre Silver Creek Ranch in 1940 for $8,000 to provide guests with fishing and hunting opportunities. By the time Janss took over the Resort, the Ranch was deteriorating from cattle grazing (which he quickly banned), overfishing, and agricultural chemicals. Unable to restore the area with his own funds, he enlisted the help of Idaho's Fish and Game Commissioner, Jack Hemingway, and others who loved the area, to sell the Ranch to the Nature Conservancy at a two-thirds market discount. Then, to help ensure the area's future protection, the group persuaded the owner of the adjacent Stalker Creek Ranch to sell his land to the Conservancy. Other landowners joined in and, today, Silver Creek is a world-class trout fishery and wildlife haunt that covers 883 acres and protects over 9,000 adjacent acres through conservation easements. It is, arguably, Blaine County's most successful land conservation project entirely dedicated to serving the public. The Nature Conservancy praises it as "one of the most successful stream conservation efforts ever undertaken."[36]

A second gift from Janss is the wide-open sweep of Sun Valley City's hillsides. In 1993, Blaine County passed an ordinance prohibiting development on County slopes with a 15-degree angle that were visible from Highway 75 — a designated scenic corridor — and 25-degree slopes visible from beyond the corridor's boundaries. The City of Sun Valley, prodded by Janss, soon followed. At first, restricting hillside development was opposed but today it is one of the more sacrosanct pieces of local legislation and the reason why most of the Valley's hills remain forested, or shaggy with rocks, or dominated by sagebrush, rather than crowded with houses, as in other resort areas. Whether the restrictions will last in perpetuity remains to be seen.

As the Valley's quality of life grew during the Janss years, so did its economy, partly due to Janss' efforts and partly due to America's booming industrial and white-collar businesses. It was the 1960s-1970s and most Americans were middle-class, confident, and looking forward to an ever-higher standard of living; they were increasingly mobile and enjoyed new-found leisure time for vacations. Janss' prediction that the ski market would boom was confirmed in the late 1960s and early 1970s when nearly half of the world's 5,500 ski areas were born. He was ready for the onslaught. In the Wood River Valley, total skier days grew from 1,000 in the 1964-65 season to 286,800 during the 1975-1976 season.

At the same time, the County's residential population more than doubled, growing from roughly 4,598 in 1960 to 9,841 in 1980. Although winter vacationers had initially provided the bulk of the Valley's earnings, many newcomers were entrepreneurial and created businesses to meet growing local needs. They joined the economy that had sprouted under Harriman — Sturtevant's (the oldest ski store in the country founded in 1948) and Michel's Christiana (a restaurant founded in 1959) — and added new businesses relevant to the evolving times: architectural firms, outfitters, art galleries, technology professionals, landscapers, and office services. Many of them are still thriving and contributing to the Valley's earnings after four or five decades: Lutz Rental (1967), Barry Peterson Jewelers (1971), Webb Landscape (1972), *Idaho Mountain Express* (1974), Evans Plumbing (1975), and Power Engineers (1975), now a global consulting firm.

Looking Forward

When he still owned the Resort, Janss once said in good humor, "Everyone I talk to thinks he owns the place." After he sold it, people still suggested improvements or asked him how he thought the new owner was doing. Janss acknowledged in an interview that he had offered a few ideas to Holding but did not hear back. It had become clear to him and others that Holding was "the man in charge;" he would run Sun Valley Resort according to his own plans. Nor would he share those plans with others, even community leaders, despite their requests.

What had been a close, mutually supportive relationship between the Resort and the Valley now seemed at risk. Holding could successfully build and operate bigger, better, and more beautiful hospitality operations than many other hoteliers, but directly enhancing community life had never been part of the equation. What, then, would be Holding's approach to the Valley?

Chapter Four

Supreme Control: Earl Holding

"Everything I ever built, I built it the best I know how."

— Earl Holding

E arl Holding came into the Valley a self-made hotelier, oil man, and landowner, born and raised in Salt Lake City's Mormon community. Tall, distinctive in appearance, and reserved in demeanor, he was a shrewd, quiet businessman who ranked #139 among America's richest and was worth $3.2 billion at his death in 2013 at the age of 86. In 2010, he had been ranked #19 on the list of the nation's private landowners with 400,000 acres grazed by 50,000 head of cattle. When he died, his business, Sinclair Oil, was the 38th largest privately held business in the United States.[37]

Holding was a private person, closely involved in managing the business opportunities he spotted. And he was terrific at spotting opportunities. In 1977, the Holdings had visited Sun Valley Resort for the first time, simply as guests. Being an inveterate builder, Holding may have imagined how he would improve the place if he owned it.

The Resort had solid bones, a European flavor, a sense of history, and a magnificent physical location.

Three months later, Holding's wife, Carol, mentioned that the Resort was for sale; a headline on the Wall Street Journal's front page read, "Disney is negotiating to buy Sun Valley." Although Holding was not a skier, he loved getting what looked like a bargain and improving on a basically sound proposition, one that he could add to his hospitality empire. When Disney backed out, Holding bought the roughly 3,500-acre Sun Valley Resort from Bill Janss after a short round of negotiations.

A Different Kind of Owner

Just as they had when Janss bought the Resort, locals worried about the new owner's intentions. For two generations, the community had looked to the Resort for jobs, visitor income, and a national, even international, reputation. In building the Resort, the two previous owners had established the Valley's image around healthy outdoor living and an egalitarian, free-wheeling culture with both a middle-class and celebrity touch. They had actively supported community interests in various ways. Would this new owner be the same? Would he care about Valley life the same way?

Locals soon learned that Holding was a different kind of man with different concerns. Harriman and Janss had been open about their plans but Holding was reticent to engage with the community about his intentions for the future. An editorial in the *Idaho Mountain Express* claimed, "The continued inability of local press or residents to get a clear picture of plans and policies in effect at Sun Valley characterize the style of management at the resort."[38] But it was pure Holding to play his cards close to his chest. A Sinclair Oil executive, who knew the man had been a skilled poker player in his youth, observed that Holding maintained the same reserve in his business life that had worked so well in his early card games.

Feeling disconnected from the Resort was a new and unpleasant experience for locals. Morale suffered and emotions gave way to anger. Locals began to imagine the worst-case scenario as they often do when left in the dark about important issues. A bumper sticker appeared around town, saying, "Earl is a four-letter word."[39] Again, the *Idaho Mountain Express* challenged Holding, writing, "In a community dominated by one employer, it is important that that employer make more than good business decisions. His business, after all, is the business of all of us. Prosperity must be considered in terms other than money."[40] Of course, it was not Holding's responsibility to broadcast his plans, but his lack of communication marked a distinct departure from the past.

Holding's Background

Uncertainty hovered for several months. Tentative answers might have emerged from Holding's business history and self-made success. Born in Utah in 1926, he had achieved great heights over many hardworking, profitable years in the hospitality and oil industries before he bought Sun Valley Resort. He had always been an independent and rather solitary, some say enigmatic, hands-on man-in-charge. Now, he was adding another property to his hospitality portfolio, the familiar niche in which he had operated for many years.

His story was one of classic American entrepreneurship. The Depression had wiped out Holding's parents, apartment caretakers, when he was just three years old. After a few years, friends of his parents (the Steven Coveys) invited them to manage an apartment complex they owned in Salt Lake City. The Holdings took the job and nine-year-old Earl maintained the yard for 15 cents an hour. Always a hard worker, he began, even in those early years, to build his fortune with sweat equity. Various reports have Holding working three hours before school, and eight hours after, for 65 cents an hour, saving

$10,000 ($180,000 today) by the time he joined the Air Force at 18. When his tour was up, his service in Europe had qualified him for tuition-free college and he enrolled at the University of Utah to earn a degree in Civil Engineering.

In 1949, after working to plant, irrigate, and harvest a fruit orchard in Dimple Dell (near Salt Lake City) with his best friend, Carol Orme, the two married. At 23, Holding was about to leave for Iran to work on water projects for the U.S. Bureau of Reclamation when the second generation of the Covey family, three brothers who owned a deteriorating 24-hour truck stop and motel in Little America, Wyoming, asked the Holdings to take over its management for a 10% stake in the business.

In 1952, the couple moved to Western Wyoming's isolated Red Desert to run the 24-hour Little America property. An unusual place to build a motel, it was where the Covey brothers had once overnighted in a blizzard to rescue sheep and they wanted to protect others from the same unpleasant experience. Holding described the motel as a small operation with a dozen rooms, a cafe with a dozen seats, a service station and slot machines sitting on the side of Highway 30 which was "not much more than a trail." However, after a year of the hands-on attention that marked the Holding's approach to business — making beds, pumping gas, registering guests — Little America began to make a profit.

In the next couple of decades, the Holdings transformed Little America into what was once said to be the highest volume service station in the United States. Gradually, the enterprising couple leveraged their earnings and properties into a major hospitality chain called Little America Hotels and Resorts. Today, it boasts eight large luxury properties in Wyoming, California, Arizona, Utah (including Snow Basin Resort), and, of course, Sun Valley Resort in Idaho.

Holding did not limit himself to hospitality interests, however. Managing that first Little America introduced him to the gas and oil industry. When premium gas for new high-compression car engines came on the market, Holding liked its profit margins. In 1958, he began wholesaling a premium blend throughout the Rocky Mountain West and, over the next decade, built a niche that dealers outside its perimeter could not penetrate. The chief executive of a Gulf Coast competitor once explained, "Shipping gasoline adds up in transportation costs. Sinclair is freed from the costs by proximity to its markets. It's a wonderful little niche market where gross profit margins run about $2.50 a barrel higher in the Rockies than in the Gulf Coast."[41]

In 1968, Holding vertically expanded his oil business by purchasing a small, about-to-close Mobil Oil refinery in Casper, Wyoming. He borrowed heavily to buy it, as entrepreneurs will do, and entered a federal subsidy program for small refiners who agreed to supply crude oil at reasonable prices. Six years later, the refinery was going strong with steady clients, including the Air Force, Union Pacific Railroad, and 1,000 service stations around the Rockies.

Holding then began some serious business expansion. In 1974, he acquired San Diego's Westgate Hotel in a bankruptcy auction. In 1976, he mortgaged his hotel properties to buy a large portion of Sinclair Oil's refining, distribution, and retail stations. He bought ranch lands in Wyoming and Montana, and real estate in Salt Lake City where, at one time, the number of properties he owned was second only to the Mormon Church. An employee of his, attuned to his interests, once gave him a plaque that read, "All I want is the land next to mine."

Holding was clearly a shrewd businessman when it came to cultivating his markets and beating out his competition. The community might have taken some solace from Holding's success, but it wanted reassurance that the friendly rapport between the Resort and the Valley would continue.

Holding's First Steps with the Resort

The community got its first inkling of Holding's plans for Sun Valley Resort from a November 1977 *Sports Illustrated* article, "I see Sun Valley as a Grande Dame that has been sitting on her laurels," he said. "There's a tremendous challenge here. We want to make this place a masterpiece again," adding, "All it takes is money and we've got that." And so he had and so he did.[41]

What Holding meant gradually unfolded. First, he ended condominium development and took the Resort's "For Sale" properties off the market. He had no interest or need to sell residences for capital or operating income — a situation appreciated by locals who had disliked Janss' ongoing development. With a fond eye for beauty, he hired landscape crews to plant more than 2,000 trees and shrubs, working right beside them. People in the community began to appreciate Holding, agreeing that the Valley was lucky to have him.

Next, Holding began to update the Resort's infrastructure and refurbish the retail stores and Opera House, replacing roofs, plumbing and irrigation. He beautified the Resort's lodging in an elegant European style with new tapestries, textured upholstery, and oak reproductions of French furniture. Only the highest quality materials were used: real leather, South American marble, brass fixtures in the bathrooms, opulent crystal chandeliers, and thick, custom-patterned wool rugs. Beauty and taste coalesced in an atmosphere that was inviting and comfortable, expensive but not ostentatious. Everything reflected the man's love for lush materials, inside and out, regardless of cost. Holding liked to do something "only once and do it right," an executive explained, "Marble lasts longer than tile, and tile lasts longer than linoleum."

The restoration was finished in a whirlwind six weeks and the Resort miraculously opened for the summer and stayed open year-round for the first time, something Janss had wanted but only Holding could afford. It became a lovely cocoon for vacationing guests, as well as for locals who could enjoy luxury at their fingertips without paying for a room. In wintertime, guests and locals could ski Baldy, classic skate on Nordic trails, snowshoe, or ride a horse-drawn sleigh to Trail Creek Cabin for dinner. They could enjoy European or American cuisine at the restaurants, followed by an after-dinner liqueur in the cozy Duchin Room with its live music and wood paneled walls. During the other three seasons, guests and locals could swim, play tennis, enjoy golf on one of several high-quality courses, shoot clay targets, horseback ride, or watch ice shows starring Olympic medalists.

What About Baldy?

Holding had never been a skier but, after buying the resort, he and Carol took lessons at Baldy's ski school with the new head instructor, Rainer Kolb, who was reputedly tough on employees but devoted to the Holdings. Despite the snowmaking recently installed by Janss on the Lower Warm Springs and Flying Squirrel runs, Holding reported in an interview, "We really skied on ice. Neither of us knew what we were doing and (at the end of the day), Carol was black and blue from falling."[43] Doubtless, this did not endear the mountain to Holding and, after a while, it seemed he was more intent on improving everything associated with the Resort, except Baldy. Just as perfecting the mountain had been Janss' Holy Grail, so were the Resort's quality and beauty for Holding.

In addition to putting Baldy on the back burner, Holding cancelled the mountain's international races, including the Harriman Cup, reportedly to avoid liability issues. But that cut the cord with national and international skiers who had helped build the Resort's reputation as a skier's paradise. Sun Valley's mayor at the time, upset that Baldy's renown was fading, warned Holding that his inattention to the mountain was harming the Valley's competitive standing with other ski resorts. "He got furious," she recalled. But she was not alone. *Idaho Mountain Express* reported a "resentment of the employees, the

Valley and the whole state" about Holding's indifference to Baldy, a mountain that, in fact, "belonged to the whole nation." The editorial pointed out that the Resort's "special use permit" from federal agencies allowed it to run a business on Baldy only if it provided the greatest amount of good for the greatest amount of people. By ignoring the mountain, Holding was hurting the tourist trade and local businesses that relied on it.

Two groups formed to protest what they believed was the Resort's failure to fulfill its permit requirements. In 1979, a group called Skiflation sued the Forest Service for approving the Resort's sudden and significant price increase for Baldy's lift tickets. The group's efforts failed, however.[44] A decade later, Restore Sun Valley's Ski Prominence (RSVP) sued Holding for "restraint of trade," arguing that the Resort had offered a low-priced room-rental/ski-free package that undercut other local hotels. It also paid employees the lowest rate in the ski industry and received income from public property without contributing to the community. If the group won the lawsuit, it intended to take over Baldy's operations, but, as with Skiflation, it lost.

By this point, it was clear that, while Holding was excellent at identifying business opportunities and successfully expanding them, he was not interested in community affairs. This was very different from the previous owners who had believed that the Resort's business was also the business of the entire community.

Holding Turns to Baldy

Fortunately, Holding finally turned his attention to Baldy. According to one story, a friend from Mammoth Mountain came to ski one day. At the top of the mountain, he looked around, turned to Holding in astonishment, and said, "You don't know what you have here." If the story is true, Holding apparently took him at his word and responded with spectacular effect.

Starting in 1990, he introduced one state-of-the-art improvement after another until Baldy began to surpass other ski mountains. He replaced slow lifts with seven high-speed quads, including the first chair to whisk skiers straight to the top of Baldy in just 10-12 minutes, half the previous time. He opened new terrain in Frenchman's, a lovely, secluded area that offered two groomed runs (one named Janss Pass) and the first groomed glade. Perhaps his most productive on-mountain investment came after several dry years in the late 1980s when he spent $16 million in the world's most advanced computerized snowmaking system, installing 38 miles of underground pipes.

In all his efforts to develop Baldy, Holding never deviated from the highest standards, regardless of cost. "It's very difficult to run a business that is so weather dependent," he once remarked to an interviewer. "When we started, the snowmaking amounted to mostly water sprayed in the air with a little air added to it but (over time) we've spent $22 or $23 million on snowmaking."[45]

Holding also constructed spectacular lodges at the base of Warm Springs and River Run, and a third lodge perched magnificently on the top of Seattle Ridge. "The mountain is regal, and it is only fitting that she wears a crown radiant with three precious jewels," observed one admirer.

Gradually, Baldy's upgrades drew favorable national attention. Media reviews praised the mountain for having the best ski and snowboard surfaces in the country. They also praised the area for its surprisingly down-to-earth atmosphere, describing Ketchum as "full of frontier charm and lively color. An odd hybrid offering the best of both worlds, it is a ski destination unlike any other."[46] The tourist trade began to pick up and the community's appreciation for Holding grew, particularly among the most ardent local skiers. He may have seemed aloof but, when he paid attention to the Resort's facilities, he did things the right way. Locals once again began to look to the Resort as the Valley's economic engine, just as they had when Harriman and Janss were the owners.

Holding's Business Style

From his first days of ownership, Holding appeared content to own an exclusive, elegant, and quiet get-away spot, run less like a business than a hobby, indulging his talents and tastes without fretting about profits. Unlike Holding, however, the Valley's small businesses still needed tourist income and they wanted the Resort to attract their potential clientele. His undeniable improvements to all parts of the Resort were offset by what locals perceived to be scant marketing, weak customer service, poor accessibility for visitors, and substandard employee management.

For marketing, the Resort promoted its heritage as "The Original Ski Resort," and suggested that visitors "Come for the Winter (and) Stay for the Summer." But locals searching for ads and promotional materials in the national media could barely find any. At one public meeting, an executive was heard to quote the marketing budget at $250,000. A Valley businessman, shaking his head, commented, "It's like falling off a log to have marketing when you have a tourism business." *Men's Journal* wrote up the mountain as a great place to ski, being virtually empty since "…money was poured into making a great mountain instead of marketing campaigns."

Many locals, and perhaps visitors as well, reported shabby customer service, despite the luxurious atmosphere. Staff rarely smiled and often seemed too busy to respond to guests' needs. Toward the end of the evening in a restaurant, diners would have to raise their voices above the clatter of chairs being put on tables. Wait staff might be unable to describe a menu item. It went against common sense that such a lovely Resort did not stress customer care.

Nor was it easy for visitors to reach the Valley. When Holding took ownership, he cancelled the Twin Falls-Ketchum bus service that

Janss had initiated. Subsequently, visitors entering or leaving the Valley often faced an endurance test. On a snowy winter day, an inbound airline flight might end in Twin Falls, followed by a three-hour bus ride to the Valley. Morning flights reversed the process, departing the Valley at 4 a.m. Again, *Men's Journal* observed, "Having once been the most accessible ski town in the country, it has become one of the least accessible...Skier numbers no longer seem to matter."[47] At one point, a few locals suggested that the Resort provide luxury bus service to and from airports, including Boise, but the idea was dismissed by management, saying "Bus service is not up the Resort's alley."

Holding also developed a reputation for being tight-fisted with employees, first evident when he rehired just half of Janss' workforce at lower wages and without ski privileges. As he and Janss had agreed, working with unions would no longer be a problem, but many locals were suddenly out of work and hurting. A few employees were rehired as managers, but most upper level staff were imported from Holding's other businesses and insufficiently trained, according to those who reported to them. One lift operator found that his new boss "was unwilling to listen to those with experience...often resulting in tricky situations that we had to cover for." A waitperson said, "No one knew who was in charge in my restaurant. If a customer complained about the food, the manager left it to the chef and wait staff to fight it out."

Over time, the Resort's management practices became a conversation topic among locals for substandard pay, tiny raises (if any), minimal training, and few, if any, promotions. The work atmosphere was dispiriting, generating frustration and frequent turn-over. One young employee who left the Resort after a year explained, "If you don't invest in training for employees or management, and you provide minimal pay, and you fill the minimal number of jobs possible, you can't expect to have high-quality employees willing to invest extra effort in their work. Imagine...a supposed quality resort without customer service."

The "stars" of the workforce had always been the ski instructors. Harriman and Janss, aided by ski luminaries Freidl Pfeiffer, Sepp Froelich, Sigi Engl, and Rainer Kolb, had built Baldy's ski school into what was often described as "the nation's finest." Instructors were treated well, had guaranteed teaching hours, and received free room and board. When Holding took over, however, much of that changed and many instructors moved on unless they owned homes and had close ties to clients who tipped well. Then, a few years ago, just before Baldy's winter season opened, work conditions changed again. Instead of a guaranteed retainer, instructors would be paid hourly for their work at a non-negotiable rate. According to one long-time instructor, "We were devastated. Many of us had invested our careers with the company. It seemed that the longer you worked for Sun Valley, the less work you got." While the quality of the remaining ski instructors was still high, the ski school's reputation diminished.

Today, a relatively small number of locals work full-time at the Resort, unlike pre-Holding years when it seemed that anyone who grew up in the Valley had worked there at one time or another. Most employees are foreign and temporary, living in America on J-1 Non-Immigrant Visas and working in low-paying short-term jobs in return for cultural exposure.[48] Many J-1s are eager for the opportunity, but the Valley's young people must look elsewhere for seasonal income.

Perhaps Holding's approach to the people aspects of a business should not have been surprising. He was a civil engineer, after all, and most engineers focus on facts, procedures, and numbers, rather than people. One time, describing himself, Holding had said, "I'm really not a joiner." Also, like many engineers, Holding could be a micro-manager, paying very close attention to how his plans were implemented. According to one resort executive, "Every decision had his finger on it." A Montana broker who worked with Holding for many years explained in an interview: "I never know when he'll call me or from where. But he manages every detail himself...It's all a one-man show."

While micromanagers usually produce high quality products, their frequent interventions can create stressful work climates. Holding's command and control style was so well-known that an *Idaho Mountain Express* humor columnist once wrote that he would like to be appointed to the Resort's Board so that, "At a high level Board meeting when everyone is saying, 'Yes, Mr. Holding,' Or 'No, Mr. Holding,' I would be there to say, 'Who's Mr. Holding?'"[49]

Holding's reserved nature, engineer's focus, and close hand with money may help explain his lack of interest in engaging the Valley community. Early on, Ed Scott (founder of Scott Sports) asked Holding for a donation to a new historical museum in Ketchum, but the billionaire declined. His reaction might have been predicted by Salt Lake City residents who, when asked for a donation, would reportedly reply, "Put me down for what Earl has given." Utah Senator Orrin Hatch, sympathizing with Holding, once suggested that the billionaire's thriftiness stemmed from his impoverished background, saying, "When you come up the hard way, and I know about this, you tend to hang onto everything you have, and you don't lose that feeling even when you've become a success. Earl invests in Earl."

Holding died in 1986 and, with his family now in charge, the Resort's working atmosphere has eased in many ways. Customer service has greatly improved. Employees appear to enjoy their work. More locals are hired for full-time jobs (32+ hours) and, while they still report low pay and non-existent training, they have health insurance, paid vacation time, a 401K, and an automatic ski pass for Baldy and the Resort's Nordic trails. They can vacation for free at any Little America hotel, enjoy a complimentary birthday dinner at Sun Valley Resort and, at Christmas, expect a $25 bonus for each year of employment. These benefits are well-appreciated by ski bums postponing a career or working a second job, and by retirees eager to keep busy or earn extra income, but the terms still offer only marginal appeal to the cadre of young career-oriented people looking to start families and build secure futures in the Valley.

The Resort's community involvement has also grown in the past few years. There are meeting room discounts for non-profit organizations, and ski pass donations to non-profit fund-raisers. The Resort also assists the local junior ski program with discount passes and tuition scholarships, as well as helping to set up and manage mountain races.

The Valley's Growing Economic Independence

Despite Holding's personal distance from the Valley community, his expenditures on Baldy meant that alpine skiing got better and better each year, even if it was not nationally advertised. For this, he was deeply appreciated by locals who enjoyed multiple runs on exquisitely groomed slopes that were virtually empty. In an article praising the Valley's beauty and the quality of Baldy's ski terrain, a reviewer for *The Washington Post* wrote in amazement, much as had *Men's Journal*, "There's almost nobody there."[50] This was great for local skiers, but Baldy's skier days remained relatively static. Between 2006 and 2017, the average number of skiers per season was around 350,000 (ranging from 331,000-421,000) at a Resort whose lifts are now capable of carrying 22,000 skiers per hour.[51]

Nevertheless, the Valley's economy kept growing and diversifying in business sectors that reflected the nation's economic and technological development. Advances in communications methods and social media made it ever more possible for business owners, location-neutral professionals, and "gig" workers to live where they wanted yet market themselves directly to their target audience and provide quality service to clients hundreds of miles away. Remember the television commercial, "Because of the way things work today, my office is everywhere"?

Whether to start their own business or employed by a distant corporation, these white collar workers came to the Valley for its scenic beauty, outdoor recreation, and authentic community, growing the population faster than any previous or following decade. As they got to work, embracing the Valley's lifestyle, they enlarged its virtual cycle of income and formed their own tight bonds with the existing community. Their skills and talents fit the new local affluence: high end furniture refinishing, manicure-pedicure shops, pet care workers, top-of-the-line sports equipment and clothing manufacturers, technology and business consultants, and a panoply of alternative health and wellness practitioners. Hispanic and Latinx entrepreneurs emerged as well. Having come to the Valley initially as service workers, many started restaurants and other businesses in landscaping, home repairs, and computer support. As the Valley's economy expanded, its profile began to change, moving past a primary reliance on tourism toward a broader portfolio of Main Street niches, of which tourism was just one part.

At the same time, the once close ties and shared interests between the Resort and the Valley began to attenuate, at least in part due to the hospitality industry explosion around the millennium (especially for luxury hotels). When Sun Valley Resort's famous history could not offset its lack of the five-star rating desired by affluent travelers, the local real estate lobby began to advocate for commercially-branded, five-star hotels that often lured second-home buyers. In essence, they advocated for competition with the Resort.

Then, the Recession hit, investment money dried up, and hotels once on the docket for approval were cancelled. The Valley suddenly had breathing room to consider its future. But little changed and, in the past few years, the call for luxury hotels has re-emerged, affirming that the Resort is no longer the anchor of the Valley's economy. Nor, perhaps, did the Holdings ever want to fill that distinct role.

A Good Investment?

Asked in 2000 if the Resort had been a good investment, Holding answered, "The bottom line is I think it was a good business decision...We own something like 2,500 or 2,800 acres...and the value has appreciated a considerable amount, but it's not a red-hot investment in comparison to other things we have. It's been a labor of love...Everything I ever built, I built it the best I know how...and I think we've helped this place."

The locally-shared belief is that Sun Valley Resort's operations relied on Sinclair Oil in the background. Certainly, Holding could advantageously treat the Resort as one leg of a three-legged investment portfolio comprised of oil, the hospitality sector, and land. Turning a profit may have been desirable, but it didn't seem necessary. One long-time dedicated skier observed, "We were lucky that the Holdings could afford to run the mountain at a loss. We were – and are - very spoiled."

If there has been one reliable source of apparent profit for the Holdings, it is the annual five-day summer business conference held by Allen and Company for media, technology, philanthropic, political, and financial luminaries. Each July since 1983, the billionaire boutique investment banker, Herb Allen, has rented the Resort as a "summer camp for billionaires" and their families. Its homey elegance, natural beauty, and quality amenities are perfect for five days of educational panels and mega-networking for many of the nation's business elite, interspersed with whitewater rafting, fishing, and playing golf.[52] The Valley's isolation has been a godsend, never a problem; attendees arrive at the small local airport by private jet or in nearby Twin Falls from where they are driven to the Valley. With locals restricted from using the facilities, the Resort becomes an exclusive, relaxing private club.

The national publicity for Allen's conference simultaneously benefits the Resort's visibility and reputation. Reporters and photographers roam the grounds hoping to snag a brief interview with a business mogul or get the scoop on a just-concluded mega-deal. Coverage by *HuffPost*, *Forbes*, *CNN*, and *CNBC* among others — all of it remarkably thin — illustrates how the convergence of wealth and power, even in an isolated mountain town, can draw national interest. As one reporter quipped, "No news is still news."

From the community's standpoint, Allen's get-togethers provide a much appreciated surge in local economic activity. A few years ago, he reportedly spent about $10 million to host his guests and their families, among other things hiring local organizers to farm out good-paying assignments to residents for baby-sitting, catering, shuttling cars, driving limousines, or guiding fishing and hiking trips. Year after year, except for the Covid-19 summer of 2020, locals have relied on Allen & Company for income that could be up to one-third of their yearly budgets. (See the back matter for a comment on Covid-19's impact). As an unexpected bonus, Allen's high-profile guests are typically unpretentious and easy-going, their presence bringing a subtle but upbeat excitement to the Valley's usually low-key atmosphere.

In Retrospect

At Sun Valley Resort's 50th Anniversary Celebration in 1986, eleven years after Holding's purchase, a Union Pacific executive visiting for the first time, looked around and said, "I think we screwed up." Before that moment, he was unaware of the magnificent Resort that Harriman had built and made famous with Union Pacific money. He could see, however, that Sun Valley Resort and its Wood River Valley home still offered a slice of heaven — seasoned by a 150-year history of beaver pelts, gold mines, hot springs baths, sheep ranching, and fantastic skiing. It had been a place of celebrity escapades and middle-class restorative vacations; a spiritual home for hippies and free-wheeling entrepreneurs; and a high-end, four-season luxury enclave for many in the top 1% of the nation's income strata. The Resort's historic glory may have faded — it was less well-known than in previous years — but it still possessed a beautiful, open landscape; a serene atmosphere; adjacent mountains and rivers for exploration and recreation; and a lively, embracing community. The Valley's authenticity was still palpable.

Meanwhile, Holding continued to build masterpieces. In 2008, he conjured his last major construction, the $14 million Sun Valley Music Pavilion for three weeks of Sun Valley Summer Symphony performances (now called the Sun Valley Music Festival) and a few weeks of other music and dance events. The eye-catching open-air bowl of 1,500 seats, 67 feet tall, is shadowed by a light-diffusing membrane supported by an exposed structure above walls of travertine rock imported from Italy's Mariotti quarry, the source of the stone used to build the Roman Coliseum. When a friend of Holding's asked him, "Why build such a grand building?" he replied, "Because we like to do good things."

During his last years of ownership, Holding shared his deep feelings for Sun Valley Resort with the public. Friends and employees attended his 80th birthday celebration in Sun Valley Inn's lovely, remodeled Limelight Room. His tall, handsome presence confined to a wheelchair by a stroke, Holding reportedly declared that as long as his family was alive, they would run the Resort. To be sure, every local in the room felt his sincerity and returned it with deep gratitude for his and his wife's dedication to preserving and maintaining the Resort and Bald Mountain. Without reservation, people respected Holding's drive to build his properties according to the highest personal standards of perfection. They understood why he had once explained to an executive questioning a golf course expansion: "Building a golf course is not about golf per se. It's not about simply being playable. It's about building a masterpiece."

The Holding family continues to own and operate Sun Valley Resort, upgrading and modernizing it in line with other contemporary luxury hotels. The Lodge's rooms and restaurants have been enlarged and refurbished. The original, intimate, wood-paneled Duchin room has been redesigned as a contemporary open-space bar with the piano set off to the side. Guests can relax in a luxurious 20,000 square foot Spa offering massage therapies, body health rituals, and wellness and healing practices. Employees are housed more comfortably in new dorms and attached single-family homes with affordable rental rates. Most recently, Baldy has opened 380 additional acres of ski terrain with a new high-speed quad and, as ever, spectacular views.

These efforts may reflect Carol Holding's interest in simply continuing to perfect a Resort that she loves in a community that loves her back. She is often seen around the Resort, as are her children, unobtrusively at work or checking on this and that. In 2019, she posted a large plaque at The Place, where employees can buy discounted meals; it reads, "Earl and I have always said that our employees are our most important guests." That same year, at a company-wide meeting, she indicated her family's commitment to run the Resort for at least another generation.

Meanwhile, recent improvements have made the Resort more competitive in the hospitality market and, certainly, more attractive for eventual sale. Recently, most of the assets of the Resort's parent company, Sinclair Oil, were sold to HollyFrontier Corporation, an independent petroleum refiner. So far, Little America Hotels, Snowmass, and Sun Valley Resort remain in the Holding family's hands. Locals hope that is where the Resort will remain. But to be sure, if anyone knows what the Holdings intend, they are being good friends in a gossipy town by keeping that knowledge private.

PART II

THE COMMUNITY

Chapter Five

The Valley Today: Quality of Life and Quality of Place

"The country town is one of the great American institutions."
—Thorstein Veblen

A verell Harriman felt magic when he stepped off the Little Zip into the golden aura of the Valley. He likely envisioned his luxury resort settling naturally and graciously into that winter wonderland, one that Bill Janss and Earl Holding eventually fell in love with as well. In the end, despite their varied temperaments, the three unwittingly collaborated to build a much beloved Resort, both for themselves and for others.

As they followed their dreams, the Valley developed its own culture alongside the Resort, relying at first on tourists and then, like most offspring, beginning to follow its own path. Today, the economy has expanded to include businesses and non-profits that reach well beyond the tourism niche. Yet the Valley still retains its magical aura, as if a crystal were hanging overhead shedding warmth and light onto a favored place. What is it about the Valley that people find so special?

The Magnificent Setting

For those who have never been here, the Wood River Valley is contained in a narrow fault running through rough, mountainous terrain in Central Idaho's Blaine County. It descends southward for roughly 60 miles, cradling within it a thin 35-mile strip of relatively isolated settlement. The Valley's contours were shaped over geologic ages by the earth's shifting crust and the carving action of the meandering Big Wood River which starts at roughly 9,000 feet near Galena Peak in the north and slips down across the southern slopes of the Sawtooth Mountains. From there, the river drops 137 miles, passing mountain peaks, forests of lodgepole pine and spruce, rounded foothills, willow fields, four towns, cultivated acreage, and horse and cattle country, before it flows onto the sagebrush steppe.

Once on the Valley floor, the Big Wood's originally braided course, now channeled and armored due to human habitation, flows through Blaine County alongside the towns of Ketchum, Sun Valley, Hailey, and Bellevue, each with its own personality. Public and privately-owned lands, still largely undeveloped, surround the towns and sprawl toward the Valley's hills on either side. A large amount of property is protected by conservation trusts, property easements, and hillside development restrictions. Eighty-two percent of the watershed is apportioned between the Bureau of Land Management, the Forest Service, and the State of Idaho. Thousands of acres of wild land are freely accessible to outdoor adventurers and recreationists, residents and visitors, families, and solitary souls, inviting wonder-filled hours or weeks of exploration. At night, it seems a person can touch the stars since the Valley is part of the Central Idaho Dark Sky Reserve, a huge expanse of natural darkness unmarred by artificial lighting.[53]

A short hike across the Valley's rising and falling lands quickly reveals its natural beauty: the soaring profiles of three mountain ranges; the glittering flash and silky burble of streams falling over rocks and grasses covering hillsides and canyons; sagebrush fields; the fragrance and colorful patterning of springtime wildflowers on a ridge; and the glistening, quiet white of winter meadows in the sun. Home to elk, deer, bear, moose, cougars, and an occasional wolf or endangered wolverine, the Valley is protected, private, and peaceful — uncontaminated by the noise and bustle of urban life. This sense of separation from the "real world" is a cherished asset for those who live here.

Nor is the Valley's beauty the only source of wonder. An eagle's high and sharp-eyed perspective would see beyond to other nearby majesties. Just past Galena Peak, 25 miles north of Ketchum, rise the peaks of the Boulder-White Clouds Wilderness; directly opposite them are the sharp crags of the younger Sawtooth Mountains, home to the headwaters of the Salmon River, Lewis and Clark's famed River of No Return. Both mountain chains, spectacular in different ways, are part of the 1,900-mile-long Rocky Mountain Range.

Directly south of the Valley, lying in flatter lands, are the meandering waters of the nationally known Silver Creek Preserve, Ernest Hemingway's favorite place to hunt ducks. From there, the Big Wood continues to flow toward the Snake River across a sagebrush prairie, an alluvial plain that covers one-fourth of Idaho.

The Towns

Most people come into the Valley from the south, near Hemingway's beloved hunting area, where there are spreading crop farms and livestock ranches. Driving north up the Valley, they might notice the absence of the motley strip development and megamalls found in so many communities across the country. National chains are rare and those that have gained entry — Starbucks, McDonalds, Subway, and Marriott — agreed to reduce their visual impact to respect the Valley's uniqueness.

As the Valley begins to narrow and climb, the first town to appear is Bellevue (population 2,486 in 2021), followed fifteen miles to the north by Hailey (population 8,931 in 2021), the wide main streets of both towns populated with one- or two-story wood or brick commercial buildings.[54] Both feel long-settled and unpretentious, still rural and Western, home to working- and middle-class folks, with a few newer subdivisions on the outskirts. Real estate here is relatively cheap compared to the rest of the Valley but still costly by national standards and, certainly, for most locals working in the service and hospitality industries. In 2019, the median sales price of a single-family home ranged from $365,000 to $392,500.[55]

Further North in mid-Valley are unincorporated lands zoned for large-acre, single-family properties. Homes here are expensive, sited along the Big Wood River's east bank which most homeowners have rip-rapped (to the Big Wood's detriment) with rock structures to protect against occasional flooding. Other well-to-do neighborhoods rise in the side canyons whose streams feed the river. The median home price in mid-valley in 2019 was $917,500.

Another few miles to the north is the entrance to Ketchum (population 2,879 in 2021), a town characterized today by Old West and contemporary styled architecture: 1880s brick or wood structures next to the stark glass and steel of the Pacific Northwest style; funky bars and designer dress shops; second-hand stores and a profusion of banks. Architectural Digest once listed it as one of the best 25 small towns in America.[56] Another review characterized it as "More understated than glitzy…with a rural flair (and) a distinctive character that sets it apart from just about every other major ski resort in the country." Yet a third described it as "full of frontier charm and lively color…an odd hybrid offering the best of both worlds." Median home prices here ranged from $600,000 to $807,500 in 2019.

Roughly a mile east of Ketchum lies the City of Sun Valley (population 1,496 in 2021), the home of Sun Valley Resort with its original

Lodge and Inn; shops and restaurants, ponds and grassy greens; and shooting range, tennis courts, and warm water pool. Close by is Dollar Mountain, a beginner's ski hill graced by Carol's Lodge at the base. In 2019 median home prices here for houses and the many condominiums, ranged from $421,500-$630,500.

The Valley to the North of Ketchum was the last section to be developed. Hulen Meadows, originally a garbage dump three miles out of town, was platted for homes between 1966 and 1972. At one time called "human ghettoes," the area is sought after today for its peaceful neighborhood setting among lovely hills. Two decades later, the undeveloped acreage between Ketchum's northern boundary and Hulen Meadows was annexed into the City for high-end properties now occupied by second-home owners. A few years after that, a three-mile stretch of farmland just above Hulen Meadows was rezoned into two- and three-acre lots. Today, the strip is informally called "millionaire's row" based on its large homes with sweeping views and median home price of $1,185,000 in 2019.

Finally, just above millionaire's row stretch the 756,000 acres of the Sawtooth National Recreation Area, home to mountain wilderness territory with deep forests, dispersed wildlife, sage flats, and the headwaters of the Salmon River.

Friendly, Diverse Community Life

The Valley's neighborly atmosphere can make it seem like one contiguous small town, although there is a tendency for those who live at the north and the south ends to stay "local," despite being just 15 miles apart on the highway. The five town and County governments usually have different priorities and no ready mechanism for collaboration. Wherever one lives, however, people are generally welcoming, upbeat, and easy-going. Trust is high and, once established, loyalties are strong. Crime is virtually non-existent. Tourists usually crowd sidewalks and roadways only in the high seasons.

Roughly half of the population has a college degree, or higher; two-thirds are liberally minded, viewed by others in Idaho (the reddest of red states) as spoiled socialists, weirdos, or snooty rich folks. A reporter from the Public Broadcasting NewsHour, which tends democratic and centrist, described the Valley as "the most NewsHour friendly" of anywhere he had visited. Nevertheless, one-third of the Valley voted Republican in the last three presidential elections.

Having chosen to live in an isolated spot in the barely known state of Idaho, most locals are strong individualists. People tend to march to their own drum, and they do it with energy and a fair share of self-esteem, often ignoring the potential benefits of compromise and concession. And yet, peoples' allegiance remains tightly bound to the community when push comes to shove. Most people operate on a first-name basis and are quick to pull together when tragedy strikes. Long-time locals rarely think in terms of social class, although newcomers in the past 20+ years tend to be a bit more snobbish.

Virtually everyone prefers the occasional challenges of mountain living to the clamor and conformity of urban confines, cherishing the Valley's lifestyle even when opting for it has meant (for some) a career shift, two jobs, or a cut in income. Many discovered the Valley on a Baldy ski vacation, after a raft or kayak run down one of the nearby whitewater rivers, or while camping, hiking, and fishing with a friend. Others arrived by accident. One restless 30-year-old from the Midwest threw a dart at a map for her next move; it landed on the Valley and she packed up and headed West. Still others live among three generations of families that have gathered over the years to be together. No matter what brought them here, everyone is into at least one, or several, types of outdoor recreation. A large number are award-winning athletes and there are dozens of Olympic medalists.

At the top of the economic hierarchy are the one percenters. The group includes a few long-term residents, full-time retirees, and second-home owners who live in upscale neighborhoods: corporate captains, happily overlooked celebrities, families anchored in old money, and entrepreneurs with fortunes from successful start-ups. Many could have chosen to live in other upscale Western towns but rejected them as crowded and urbanized compared to the Valley which, despite eighty years as a prestigious ski destination, still feels rural, quiet, and real.

The bulk of this group are civic-minded and support at least one or more of the 100+ registered non-profits devoted to the arts, social services, and conservation causes with their time, talents, money, or anything else they've got. Several philanthropists, working quietly but steadily from behind the scenes, have helped to build the Valley's quality of life. A fund raiser at a gracious home often includes donors with deep and not-so-deep pockets, casually dressed, drifting among tapestry covered chairs and an interesting art collection, discussing ski conditions, an aging dog's diet, or national politics. As guests fill their plates with food from bustling caterers, they might be followed by a golden retriever or mixed breed terrier looking for a handout. Donations are desired, but never pressed. A newcomer would quickly realize that, other than the size of a person's home and non-profit donations, many of the Valley's most privileged homeowners are low-key and low-profile.

The middle-class segment of the hierarchy consists largely of "old-timers," locals who were born in the Valley or Idaho or moved to the area in the 1960s and 1970s to be ski bums. Newly graduated from college and yearning to drop out for a while, they lived "rough" in Lefty's Cabins, Antlers Hotel, and Tequila Flats, "willing to be stacked like cordwood for sleeping—just for a chance to live the dream in world-famous Sun Valley." As for romance in those hippie days, a visiting New Zealander exclaimed that what happens in New Zealand in a month happens in Whistler in a week and in one night in Sun Valley!

Somewhere along the way, often after working at the Resort for a while, these contemporary "settlers" decided to stay in the

Valley, despite the tough times when snow stopped falling (April to Memorial Day) and visitors disappeared. Local incomes shrank and the towns emptied out, but, with only light work at hand, it was time to get back to the woods, the mountains and the rivers, and to play with friends. Creative and self-reliant, this group eventually expanded the economy with new businesses, helped to shape the Valley's culture, and created a broader tax base. They ran for office, joined the arts community, and founded local non-profits. Some earned professional degrees elsewhere before returning to the place they loved. Their kids attended local schools, played together on sports teams, went to the same doctors for medical care, and attended each other's birthday parties, cementing generational ties that still exist today.

Now, facing retirement or considering it, these long-term locals live in homes they have owned for years on comfortable incomes, or just enough to get by. Many of them can still be found on a winter's day gracefully ripping down Baldy at 60, and 70, and 80 years of age. They are the people who poured new oxygen into the Valley's atmosphere in Harriman's time and continued to do so for decades after, sustaining the free-wheeling, authentic, and humanistic atmosphere of today.

A third segment of the Valley's population consists of the blue- and white-collar Anglo and Latinx employees who provide the ready minds and hands that sustain Valley businesses throughout the year. The Valley could not survive without them as office administrators, labor crews, bank tellers, restaurant wait staff, firefighters, caretakers, store clerks, housekeepers, and plumbers. About half live in Hailey or Bellevue where rent is (relatively) more affordable, commuting to the North Valley for work. The rest live outside the Valley and are driven to work via van pools organized by the bigger employers. For those who drive themselves, the round-trip drive is time-consuming and costly, but at least the views in slow traffic include mountain peaks and a sapphire blue sky that might be painted with clouds, rainbows, or a sunset.

The smallest segment of the population are the agriculturalists who live and work on 236,000 acres of farms and ranches in the southern part of the Valley, an area called The Triangle. There, they grow barley and alfalfa, raise sheep and cattle, and provide a tangible taste of the Valley's Western heritage while also participating in politics and other aspects of local life. Although their numbers are relatively small, the agricultural sector and its impact are broad. Applying their energy and eco-friendly ethic, they have created a strong and growing organic food movement, set up seasonal farmer's markets, created campaigns to "buy local," and organized a regional food network.

The Valley's four towns are recreationally tied together from north to south by the Wood River Trail, 20 miles of a paved mixed-use path that runs on the old route of the Union Pacific, parallel to the Big Wood River.[57] The community is also bound together by its social infrastructure: a medical center (part of a regional system); free community-supported hospice with trained volunteers; and seven different faith communities. High quality educational programs are prominent enough to have attracted families from larger cities. The public schools enroll 40% Latinx children and offer dual immersion classes in the lower grades. Several progressive schools that follow different educational philosophies contribute to the mix. For adults, a nearby community college offers continuing education and college credits toward degrees. Otherwise, Boise State University is about a three-hour drive across the beautiful Camas prairie.

The community revels in year-round performing arts and cultural programs that nurture the Valley's intellect and imagination. Several theater groups offer high-quality comedy, drama, and musical productions; scores of art galleries show talented local and regional artists. Annual cultural events include a writer's conference with award-winning authors; a summer symphony with musicians from America's best orchestras; a wellness festival with nationally-known speakers; and a Jazz Festival that lures baby boomers from far and wide for swing, zydeco, and the blues. Finally, the Valley's revered western heritage is grandly celebrated with Fourth of July parades and fireworks, Wagon Days (celebrating the mining era), and the Trailing of the Sheep (providing a taste of the Valley's sheep-herding past).

But a Challenged Economy

The overt pleasures and beauties of Valley life tend to obscure an increasingly challenged and vulnerable economy. Today, what was once a mostly working- and middle-class community reflects the national trend toward an ever increasing wealth divide. Although the local business world has more start-ups than ever before, offering better pay than service jobs, the increased cost of living caused by growing overall wealth means that many working folks struggle to keep a roof over their heads. In 2015, the Economic Policy Institute reported that Blaine County had the greatest wealth disparity in Idaho with the top one percent earning, on average, $3.6 million per year, nearly 47 times more than the other 99% who earned roughly $77,353.[58]

In 2018, *Data USA* reported that the Valley's median household income was roughly $52,000 compared to the national norm of $62,000.[59] In 2019, the United States Census reported a somewhat higher figure with a local median household income of $56,694. Different sites report different figures at different times, but a low median wage is consistent. In fact, wages in the Valley's leisure and hospitality industry remained relatively static between 2010 and 2017 while sales increased by nearly $200 million.[59]

The result is that 38% of households in the Valley are at poverty level or struggling to meet basic needs. In each of the last three years, the Hunger Coalition has fed 20% of the local population. Yet, the focus on a tourist economy and its low-paying jobs continues despite the need for jobs that offer decent pay, training, and the potential for advancement.

Creating affordable housing to meet employee needs, whether blue- or white-collar workers, has, unfortunately, been ignored for decades. A housing assessment in 1990 by a Colorado consulting firm concluded: "The valley needs a mix of housing types; too many people are paying more than 30% of their monthly income in housing costs; and developers should be required or encouraged to set aside a percentage of newly developed homes for workforce housing." But that has rarely happened. Alternatively, developers are supposed to pay "in lieu" funds to an affordable housing account, but the requirement is often waived or reduced. Affordable housing funds have also been diverted to other purposes, as we shall see in the next chapter. The result is a crisis in middle- and working-class housing.

Today, many businesses, especially hotels, import employees from other towns or rent mobile homes for local housing. Of the roughly 21,000 Valley residents in 2019, at least 37%-40% of those who rent or own homes are "housing burdened," paying more than one-third of their income for a place to live. In 2017, the United States average cost of living index was 100 compared to the Valley's index of 126, largely due to real estate prices. In 2020, the website, Zillow, reported the County's median home value to be roughly $626,000, well over twice the national average of $226,800, and completely out-of-reach for the average local worker.[61]

These numbers will only worsen as homeowners continue to join Airbnb and VRBO programs, converting housing they once rented at reasonable rates to full time locals into expensive short-term rentals for visitors. This, of course, is happening across the United States but is especially problematic in a service-based economy that has overlooked affordable housing needs for so long. In the opinion of a Valley official involved with affordable housing, "Breaking the power structure that tilts housing away from the local community would be a big step forward in solving the housing shortage."[62] A major pillar in that structure is the real estate lobby, which favors lucrative commercial and second home development over community housing. Another pillar is the Idaho Legislature which prohibits solutions like the real estate transfer tax allowed by other states. If the situation does not change soon, the Valley's quality of life will decline significantly.

At this point, the wealth gap and its effect on housing have caused the labor force to shrink. According to the *Idaho Mountain Express*, Blaine County's 35-54 year old population, those of prime working age, dropped from 36% to 27% between 2000 and 2017, most having left the Valley for more prosperous lives elsewhere. The employees who stay often work two or three jobs and still struggle. As the employee base shrinks, employers cannot find workers, small business growth is stymied, and owners speak openly about not been able to make a reasonable living.[63] Meanwhile, the 65-plus demographic has increased 140% since 2000; of these, many no longer work, and live on fixed incomes. Increasingly worried about the escalating cost of living, they fear potential homelessness. Many of them may also need eldercare services that no one will be around to provide.

At one time, Twin Falls, a metro area 80 miles away, was a ready source of employees, but years of forward-thinking economic development by that city, including successful urban renewal planning, have built a boom town. Most of the city's residents now choose to work close to their homes where they can earn good wages, build a more certain future, and enjoy more time with their families. (The Wood River Valley would do well to learn from the growing economic success of what might be viewed as a "less sophisticated" neighbor).

If the Valley maintains its current trajectory, it might become like the "Lost People of Mountain Village," a 20-minute black and white "mockumentary" of a deserted mountain community dominated by second homeowner mansions. It opens with a backcountry skier stumbling onto "an intact relic of a very recent history, a mountain town of "unprecedented wealth and power…with outsized architecture and a lavish use of natural resources." An "archeologist" concludes it was once "a dominant civilization, inhabited by Sunset Man in its final state of decay." The community had driven real estate prices so high that workers were forced to leave, and local businesses failed. An "historian" looks at the empty streets and concludes that the wealthy eventually left too, having realized that "Mountain Village was…just a land with a tasteless display of wealth that lacked a soul."[64]

In many ways, the City of Sun Valley's Elkhorn area already feels like Mountain Village, dominated by second-home condominiums in an out-of-the-way location that lacks character, a sense of history, and the vibrations of daily life that bring a neighborhood alive. Other upscale subdivisions in the County similarly feel like outdoor mausoleums during much of the year. Is it possible that this is where the Valley is headed, given second home ownership at 60% in Ketchum and 80% in the City of Sun Valley?

Adding It All Up

The Wood River Valley is a paradise for those with the good fortune, available time, and adventurous spirit to find and enjoy it. It also helps to have money. At the same time, the Valley presents growing challenges for many locals with each passing year. Still, for the most part, people inevitably agree: "We are lucky to have found this place." And, if they ever forget what they have, they will be reminded by the visiting artists, speakers, educators, and musicians who greet their audiences with wide-eyed enthusiasm for the Valley's special aura, and praise for its warm, welcoming community.

Timothy Egan, a *New York Times* reporter, once described the Valley this way: "Despite a preponderance of $4 million homes, espresso cafes and galleries run by people with European accents, this golden mountain community still prefers to think of itself as somewhat of an Old West geezer in need of a bath and a shot of bourbon."[65] Egan exaggerated a bit, but he was not far off. The scent of old west "gee-zerdom" still lingers in the Valley 130 years after the Western frontier was declared "closed" by the federal government, and 80 years after the Resort's Grande Dame was built. Time's inexorable march always brings change, but change can be constructive if it is thoughtfully handled by forward thinkers.

The question for the Valley now is how to work with the inevitability of change in a way that still preserves that cherished "Old West" scent, distilled in a wild territory of spectacular beauty, for at least a couple more generations, despite social and political pressures otherwise. We need to identify a path forward that is appropriate to both our history and current times. And we need to learn from the many mistakes we have made during the past years of attempted economic development described in the next chapter.

Chapter Six

Economic Development Limbo

*"You cannot swim for new horizons until you have
courage to lose sight of the shore."*

—William Faulkner

I
n the Valley, we often talk about economic growth and economic
development as if they were the same. But they are not. "Growth"
is about a community's numbers: crime rate, unemployment, cost
of housing, and available labor force, among others; growth relies on
"hard data" and statistics. In the Valley's focus on tourism, for example, we count tourist numbers, tourist dollars, tourist days, and income
from Local Option Taxes.

"Development" includes growth but takes a broader perspective,
focusing on a community's 360 degree quality of life. It uses "soft
data" — impressions and opinions — to evaluate local socioeconomic
health: the educational system, medical care, social services, leadership effectiveness, and personal satisfaction, for example. The International Economic Development Council defines economic development

as "Seeking to improve the economic well-being and quality of life for a community."[66] Often, the measure of economic development is called "the happiness index."

Since at least the 1990s, Valley leadership has focused on numbers tied to tourism while overlooking broader aspects of economic development. For example, there is scant information about the rest of the small business world: their various niches, what they earn, the range and quality of their jobs, what is working and not working for owners, or how to expand Main Street's success. Nor do we evaluate the qualitative contributions of the small business world to the community's historic image, everyday lifestyle, and general health and welfare. This knowledge would give us a better grip on the community's overall development needs.

The lack of information seems odd. Even if tourism comprised most of the economy, why would the Valley's leaders ignore all other economic niches that affect our quality of life? Why would we not support their growth, rather than just tourism? But that has not happened, despite years of worrying about the Valley's economy.

Years of Worry

As far back as 1997 when the Sun Valley/Ketchum Chamber of Commerce held its annual retreat, a board member asked if relying on tourism, with its cyclical nature, was an effective strategy for the future. Would encouraging greater business diversity help guarantee a more stable economy? The idea sparked interest and a few members volunteered to explore it and report back at the next retreat.

At the 1998 meeting, the agenda included building entrepreneurship, balancing tourist- and non-tourist businesses, and promoting cooperation across Main Street. At one point, Sun Valley Resort's representative (absent from the previous retreat) asked why the group was talking about entrepreneurs and economic diversity when tourism was the Valley's one and only industry. Suddenly, the Board went silent.

Apparently unwilling to challenge the Resort's general manager and, perhaps, lacking adequate knowledge that business diversity was necessary for a community's well-being, the subject was dropped.[67]

While it made sense that the Resort's representative would push for a singular commitment to tourism, it was surprising that no one else questioned the idea. Despite the Chamber's purpose to provide the healthiest possible environment for its member businesses and the community, the Board acquiesced and approved a budget for marketing to vacationers.

That same year, the Big and Little Wood River Valley Action Plan Group (WwRAP) formed to address what seemed like out-of-control growth. An *Idaho Mountain Express* columnist described a kind of "schizophrenia" in the Valley with people torn between "little or go-slow growth and those dreaming of the sound of hammers building yet more new homes and businesses."[68] Members of WwRAP feared that the Valley's authenticity and charm were disappearing. Old buildings and small clapboard homes were being replaced by large brick, and glass and steel, structures. Second home growth was accelerating but their subdivisions were like ghost towns much of the year.

Working with an outside consultant, WwRAP surveyed the community to identify what people wanted for the future. Answers included "a caring small-town atmosphere (and) a community rich in character and culture" with economic diversity, open space, a healthy environment, a public transportation network, and managed growth.[69] Building the tourist trade was not on the list. (One gentleman even suggested that the Valley's future depended more on non-tourist than tourist businesses).

In a public review of the survey's results, WwRAP's consultant suggested that the Valley's schizophrenia might stem from "urban denial," a dynamic he had seen in mountain communities avoiding the realities of growth. "Until there's a crisis, people don't worry—they're not moved to act," he explained, urging the group to come up with an economic development plan that would preserve the community's quality of life. (If the team formed, I could find no mention of it.)

National and local crises did, indeed, occur, one after the other with ever more disruptive effects on the Valley's well-being. The national economy collapsed in the dot.com bubble of 1999-2001. On 9/11/2001, the World Trade Center fell under the impact of terrorist-controlled airplanes and Americans shunned air travel, especially vacation trips. Then, gas prices spiked for several years, curtailing gasoline-dependent travel. Finally, 2008 brought the Great Recession with its financial and housing collapse that disrupted most Americans' daily life, and that of the Wood River Valley. The local economy softened dramatically.

Mother Nature also made her voice heard. In August 2007, the heavy smoke of the three-week Castle Rock fire rendered the Valley barely habitable for anyone; several residents lost their homes. The fire was followed by a few skimpy snow seasons when the usual visiting skiers stayed home or went to other resorts. Finally, in the summer of 2013, the Beaver Creek Fire spread its arms far and wide to claim over 100,000 acres in Wood River's South Valley and a significant amount of the needed and widely anticipated high-season tourist income.

That the Valley's economy needed help became most apparent in 2000 when population growth slowed substantially. In the previous decade, the County's population had expanded from roughly 13,500 to 19,000. By 2010, however, it had added only 2,000 more residents. Ketchum's population declined by nearly 20% between 2000 and 2010 from 3,003 residents to 2,689 as people left the Valley or moved to Hailey where homes were more affordable. Many college-educated ski bums left the Valley to find better-paying work elsewhere. And, as residents were leaving the Valley, fewer tourists were showing up to keep the economy going,

Second-home owners were affected as well. Many put their homes on the market at prices lower than the original construction costs. The majority visited far less frequently. Ketchum's property tax rolls lost $600 million from 2007 to 2010. Income from building permit fees plummeted from $75 million in 2005 to under $15 million in 2010. Only Hailey's tax rolls expanded with the influx of North Valley residents, the population there increasing from 6,200 to nearly 8,000 residents between 2000 and 2010.

During these challenging times, most small business owners, tourism-based and otherwise, worried and scrimped their way toward the future. Others failed or uprooted for more dynamic business environments. The lesson learned by some, but not all, was that towns that rely on just one business niche were economically vulnerable. A local business owner pointed out, "In a one-product economy, if that product gets damaged, everybody's in trouble. If we do not wake up and watch how we're doing business, we may not be around."[70]

Need for Economic Diversity Is Ignored

Between 2001 and 2010, different Valley organizations hired outside consultants to identify how to strengthen the struggling economy. Each group of experts validated what the Sun Valley/Ketchum Chamber of Commerce had intuited in 1997: a strong economy required business diversity, especially entrepreneurial activity, to provide year-round employment, well-paying jobs, and the innovative culture that spawns vitality and new business growth.

The Chamber of Commerce commissioned the first study in 2001, hiring Dean Runyan Associates to identify how much money visitors had contributed to local earnings between 1990 and 2000. In an "Economic Analysis of Blaine County," Dean Runyan determined that short-term visitors had provided roughly 30% of earnings, vacation-home owners another 27%, and full-time residents the balance of 43%.[71] Thus, short-term tourism was important to the Valley, but it was not dominant. Nearly half of the earnings came from full-time residents. (Since Dean Runyan's report, claims are often made that two-thirds of the local economy depends on tourists. I can't find the source of that number but it may come from conflating short-term visitor earnings with those from long-term vacation homeowners.)

In 2007, the Southern Idaho Economic Development Organization commissioned a planning study for its region. The report described Blaine County as "...changing from a seasonal resort area to a...diversified economy less impacted by the seasons."[72] That same year, the County hired Claggett Wolfe Associates to study the market feasibility of a business incubator. It concluded that the Valley's "successful and burgeoning entrepreneurs...could benefit from business development programs."[73] Finally, in 2009, the County hired Theory Into Practice Strategies (TIPS) to propose a strategy that would ensure the County's economic vitality. TIPS' recommendations included the need to diversify the economy beyond tourism and second-home sales, and to support small business and entrepreneurial growth.[74] All together, these studies cost the Valley over $200,000.

Interestingly, a side issue about Valley leadership was highlighted in all four studies. Claggett Wolfe described it best: "Leadership in the County appears to be fragmented with various groups pulling in different directions and competing for economic development resources and funding." But leaders already knew that was happening. Just prior to the studies, the cities had hired an outside consultant to help them improve their collaboration. After that, a few monthly joint meetings were held but soon faded out. (Ironically, back in 1902, a letter to the Ketchum Keystone editor had suggested, "More people will come to the valley if the valley is more unified in its outreach.")

The failure of the community to follow through on what so many economic experts had suggested was highlighted at a Valley-wide business conference several years later. In 2013, the managing partner of TIPS was invited back to give the keynote speech. Before an audience of 200 or so business leaders, he firmly, and somewhat ruefully, observed that none of TIPS' recommendations had been implemented. The status quo had prevailed.

Ketchum Struggles with Urban Renewal

Meanwhile, during the same troubling years, Ketchum took a different approach to economic development. In 2005, the City's commercial core was struggling. Retail businesses were closing, sales tax income was down, residential construction was taking over, and street life was virtually non-existent. Rather than commissioning a study, the City Council hired The Hudson Company (Hudson) out of Moscow, Idaho to take charge of economic recovery.

One of Hudson's first impressions was that Ketchum's "year-round middle class (was) actively engaged in leaving...You're losing your sense of community...and there is no common vision."[75] He then organized a community process to design a "Town Plaza" a public area with seating, trees and grass, chess tables, an ice cream stand, and a performance stage. The Plaza would be edged by small businesses and affordable housing; sculptures would decorate the sidewalks. It would become the heart of the City; and donations to build it flowed from the community.

Hudson also suggested Ketchum implement a federal program called Urban Renewal. The details were complex but cities and towns across the country had used it to convert impoverished, crime-ridden neighborhoods into thriving mixed-use developments. Small businesses had received capital infusions, infrastructure had been repaired, crime had been curtailed, and affordable housing had been built.

On the other hand, governments had sometimes abused the program to benefit private, rather than public, interests. A posh golf course in Palm Springs received over $16 million for further embellishments and, in Denver, a $9 million nine-acre parcel of land was sold to a developer for $30. In one sweeping decision, California's

Supreme Court shut down its massive Urban Renewal program (400 agencies) because it had created a huge state deficit.

The City Council liked Hudson's ideas and formed the Ketchum Urban Renewal Agency (KURA) to address "economic underdevelopment and provide affordable housing in blighted areas."[76] The Agency would shut down after 24 years, per government rules, terminating in 2030. Any development debt incurred by the KURA would be repaid through Tax Increment Financing (TIF), an urban renewal mechanism in which the yearly increment in taxes stemming from a property's improvement was returned directly to the KURA, rather than being shared with other taxing districts. The Council may have relied on Hudson to guide the implementation of urban renewal, rather than learn about it themselves, but one way or the other, their decisions created several problems, as we shall see.

The Council's first step was to appoint itself, and only itself, to serve as the Urban Renewal Agency's Board. This was immediately problematic. Such boards are meant to have just one or two Council members, plus a few politically independent volunteers with relevant skills to avoid bias and conflicts of interest in decision-making. Other Idaho towns with urban renewal programs — Eagle, Sandpoint, Garden City, and Post Falls — had followed these standards. Nevertheless, Ketchum pushed ahead, its lawyer also representing both the City and the Urban Renewal Agency.

Next, the "Council/Urban Renewal Board" cited 10% of Ketchum's properties as blighted, another federal requirement. This included roughly 800 parcels, including Baldy's Warm Springs base and the Warm Springs Ranch where luxury residential and hotel development had already been approved. The designations were surprising for anywhere in the upscale Ketchum, but particularly for properties deemed suitable for resort living. The Council/Urban Renewal Board then changed its goals from "addressing economic underdevelopment and affordable housing" to "creating a stronger resort presence."

Next, the Council/Urban Renewal Board took out three loans totaling $5.56 million to start development, plus another $640,000 from Ketchum's in-lieu affordable housing fund (without a payment schedule or pay-off date).[77] The money would enable development to start immediately, even though there was no TIF income on hand to repay the loans.

Ketchum's immediate assumption of heavy debt was contrary to other urban renewal agencies that had chosen to bank some amount of TIF income before starting development.[78] Again, Idaho's Sandpoint, Eagle, and Garden City had done this, as did Hailey when it implemented urban renewal a few years later.

Ketchum soon learned it had made a big mistake. The Great Recession began in 2008, and the Valley's economy was hit hard. Tourism died. Property values dropped precipitously. Pending construction loans were cancelled and a host of North Valley construction projects disappeared, including four hotels, two of them on "blighted" sites. Hailey's economy also suffered when three large residential developments were cancelled. An article in the *Idaho Mountain Express* lamented, "The economic recession hit the reset button on 20 years of steady housing and population growth in Blaine County."[79]

Suddenly, the Council/Urban Renewal Board found itself holding deeply devalued properties, with little or no income on the horizon, a large amount of debt, and no cash savings. What had looked like a great approach to economic development had imploded.

The Resort to the Rescue?

Then, in 2009, Sun Valley Resort asked the Council/Urban Renewal Board to annex its 138-acre River Run ski base. It had wanted to expand River Run for years and the time seemed right. The site already had a lodge, restaurant, and retail stores to which it would add a 10-story, five-star hotel with 180 rooms, 520 residences, and 35,000 square feet of restaurant and retail space that would greatly increase Ketchum's sales tax receipts.[80]

At public hearings, locals voiced three major objections: River Run's commercial expansion would compete with Ketchum's business core; the development posed environmental concerns; and the hotel's proposed height would exceed established planning and zoning regulations designed to preserve the City's character. Nevertheless, River Run was subsequently annexed with the $3 million annexation fee waived since Ketchum's tax receipts would be so healthy.

Then, River Run was designated a blighted area by the Council/Urban Renewal Board, this time for its potential to boost Ketchum's real estate (TIF) income. Estimates had come in from two consultants (one paid by the Resort, the other by Ketchum) that River Run's development would provide $25 million in TIF money to Ketchum for the next 13 years plus $3.6 million annually for seven years after that (roughly $50 million in total over the remaining 20 years of the urban renewal program).[81] Unfortunately, the Resort's General Manager had publicly warned the City that River Run would not be developed for another 7-10 years, leaving just 10 years (not 20) to collect TIF income.

Today, more than a decade after River Run was annexed and declared a blighted area, there is no hint of impending development. On one hand, Ketchum's commercial core has been free of competition from Resort businesses; on the other, the City has received no income to offset the $3 million waived annexation fee. Finally, in 2017, Ketchum's Finance Director corrected the 2010 estimates for TIF income from River Run's development. Instead of $50 million, Ketchum's urban renewal fund will likely receive just $10 million-$18 million.[82]

A Bad Couple of Years for Main Street

Although Main Street had escaped unwanted competition from River Run, its interests were soon undermined by two other events.

The first was the dissolution of the Sun Valley/Ketchum Chamber of Commerce by government leaders. The process began with three more economic studies by a few Valley residents. First, a Sun Valley City Councilor, concerned about the City's declining income, graphed Local Option Tax (LOT) revenues for the Sun Valley Resort Area for the previous nine years and revealed a sharp downward trend. (Local Option Taxes are collected by resort areas to pay for infrastructure needs that stem from tourism). In a second study, he compared Blaine County's earnings to Colorado's resort-oriented Pitkin and Teton Counties and showed that their earnings came from 10 business niches while Blaine County relied on just three: construction, real estate, and retail trade. In line with earlier studies by outside consultants, he concluded, "Economic diversity is critical to the long-term prosperity of proprietors and earners in a resort economy. Ultimately, however, he called for more hotels.[83] (The *Idaho Mountain Express* noted the study in an article titled, "The Cleveland of Mountain Towns.")[84]

Then, another group, the Sun Valley/Ketchum Independent Marketing Committee, formed to conduct its own study. It, too, agreed with the need for greater business diversity and also decided that the Valley should rely less on second home construction, provide better visitor access and better marketing of the community's unique qualities, and build more four- and five-star hotels. Faced with these diverse findings, the Marketing Committee made just one recommendation: Build more high-end hotels to attract more tourists.[85] Finally, it called for replacing the name "Ketchum" with "Sun Valley" in all marketing campaigns.[86]

Then, the Marketing Committee criticized the Chamber of Commerce for ineffective marketing campaigns that had "failed to differentiate the resort area from its competitors." Its solution was to replace the Chamber — the advocate and service provider for Main Street — with a new organization, the Sun Valley Marketing Alliance, which would have just one mission: to market to tourists. Once again, tourism was reflexively seen as the only source of economic and community welfare.

The business community opposed the Marketing Committee's solution but, after months of turmoil between Sun Valley and Ketchum governments, the Marketing Alliance got the nod.[87] It took a year to get up and running and initially offered a few business services, but they soon disappeared. Since then, the organization (better known as Visit Sun Valley) has had several directors, an annual budget that typically runs about $400,000-$440,000, and produced no data showing its return on investment. This is one of the organizations that claims two-thirds of the Valley's income derives from visitors.

The second time Main Street was undermined was when Ketchum's Council/Urban Renewal Board approved a Starbucks Heritage Cafe for the Town Plaza, again despite Main Street's opposition. In February 2011, the Board had published a Request for Proposals (RFP) to open a "food service" business in the empty Town Plaza building that had been bought for affordable housing with affordable housing funds.[88] The RFP was unusually specific and had a short two-week deadline. When just one proposal was submitted by a recently formed, (although as yet unincorporated) Cairde Group, it seemed that Starbucks would soon be approved.

Then, a back story emerged. Two years earlier, Starbucks representatives had talked with the City's Mayor and its Director of Economic Development about renting the Town Plaza building when it became available. Starbucks was already on Main Street but rarely occupied and it wanted a more prominent site.[89] Hence, the RFP's call for a "food service" business. When asked about the RFP's specific focus and short timeline, the Director explained that an opportunity had presented itself and she had done what she could "to make it fair."[90] Main Street, especially the coffee shops, did not think the RFP was fair, however. Nor did those who knew the building had been bought for affordable housing with public funds.

After learning the back story, 30 businesses organized as the Ketchum Business Group and lobbied for a new RFP without the food service requirement. Ketchum complied but with an even shorter submission period. At the public hearing to award the contract, the room was crammed with small business owners. Cairde Group representatives were absent, however, so Ketchum's Mayor volunteered to read its proposal for a Starbucks shop with a Visitor's Center: a wall nook with promotional brochures and an information agent perched nearby on a stool. There would also be TV monitors showing promotional videos for Ketchum.

The Ketchum Business Group then proposed a Visitor's Center for the entire site. Volunteers would greet people, show them around, and answer questions about events, adventure trips, gallery walks, and local history, among others. The walls would be covered with information brochures, profiles of small business owners, and video portraits of the Valley's lifestyle characteristics. Visitors could relax in comfy chairs with a cup of coffee and watch kids play in a roped-off area. The operation would be community run and self-supporting.

The presentations were barely over when the Council/Urban Renewal Board announced that Starbucks had won the space. For some, the decision was a surprise, but it was only those who had missed the mayor's announcement prior to the presentations that a decision had already been made.

During subsequent lease negotiations with Starbucks, Ketchum approved a low-rate, five-year lease with the option to renew for two additional five-year periods. It also agreed to pay $120,000 toward the building's remodel as well as the yearly maintenance of the Visitor's Center, public lavatory, and free seating for customers on the Town Plaza. Finally, if Ketchum wanted to terminate Starbucks' lease early, it would have to provide a year's notice and pay the corporation

$100,000. As promised, TV monitors were installed to show the $500,000 worth of promotional videos for Ketchum as "The Original Mountain Town," but they were soon muted because the sound disturbed Starbucks' customers. Then, the videos disappeared altogether.

All Those Economic Development Organizations

In 2010, the *Idaho Mountain Express* carried an article titled, "Just Get it Done" about the number of economic development organizations in the Valley and their lack of coordination and accomplishments.[91] The proliferation had occurred during the decade of economic development studies, but to little effect. Everyone wanted economic development but couldn't pull together on what it should look like and how to get there. Two of the organizations are still active.

The first is the Ketchum Community Development Corporation (KCDC), founded with the urban renewal program to partner in small business and affordable housing development.[92] Hudson, the consultant who had suggested the organization, was hired by the Council for $200,000/year to run it; after public opposition to his salary, however, he resigned. Two more directors were hired and let go over the next three years. The fourth, hired in 2010, was a local news reporter praised for his youthful enthusiasm but lacking any background in economic development. This became apparent when the Twin Falls office of the U.S. Department of Agriculture granted the KCDC a $100,000 revolving loan fund to assist business start-ups. It failed to make a single loan during the following year, however, and the grant was withdrawn. (Fortunately for one hopeful entrepreneur, the Twin Falls office had its own revolving loan fund. After being rejected by the KCDC, she successfully applied there and has run a retail business on Ketchum's Main Street for the past ten years.)

In 2014, the KCDC took the initiative to open a business incubator, an idea popular around the United States. It was called the Ketchum Innovation Center and was well-received. Over the next few years, it provided a few start-ups with office space, pitch opportunities to investors, mentoring, lunch talks, and networking opportunities. It had its own difficulties, however, including little evidence of a return on investment, and eventually closed after two more directors came and went.[93]

Meanwhile, the Innovation Center's parent, the KCDC, had begun to fade into the background. Today, it has a four member Board and no paid positions. The Mayor, who is not on the Board, is the usual spokesperson when the KCDC does occasionally act. A recent check with Charity Navigator, an organization that evaluates the financial health of non-profits, gives the KCDC a failing score for financial stability, efficiency, and sustainability.[94]

The second economic development agency that is still operating is Sun Valley Economic Development (SVED), also formed in 2010. SVED is best known for its yearly Economic Summit with guest speakers addressing topics such as national trends in housing and travel, community resilience, and what makes a town lively. SVED is also known for presenting annual performance data for eight Valley industries: Construction, Professional, Leisure/Hospitality, Government, Trade/Transportation, Education/Health, Finance, and Miscellaneous. But it has yet to provide data about the sub niches within each industry and their economic impacts on the Valley. Nor has SVED gathered data about local self-employed entrepreneurs, of which there are many.

The organization's current mission is to attract, retain, and develop small businesses, but data is unavailable about its results.[95] The good news is that retaining and developing start-ups is a gaining strategy in small towns across the country; the bad news is that attracting businesses has lost favor. Further, luring businesses to the Valley would seem nearly impossible given the high cost of living, lack of affordable housing, transportation challenges, and shrinking employee base.

Today, SVED continues to describe the local economy as two-thirds dependent on tourism, almost 20 years after the claim was first made. It is time for the economic development group to either revalidate or update the numbers. In doing so, SVED must reconsider how it calculates who actually contributes what to the economy. In fact, locals and their families patronize tourist businesses and pay Local Option Taxes but their economic impact is automatically attributed to tourism.

Evaluation of Ketchum's Urban Renewal Program

By 2015, the dysfunction of Ketchum's Council/KURA Board was obvious enough to attract close scrutiny. In a five-hour meeting among Council/KURA Board members, staff and other advisors, and a lawyer specializing in urban renewal, several problems were identified.[96] The organization's leaders had purchased unprofitable properties; relied on inflated financial projections; used affordable housing funds for urban renewal projects and not yet repaid the debt; played dual roles; and had incurred debt payments that exceeded its income. The Director of the KCDC at the time further noted that, "The Ketchum City Council, the URA and the Community Development Corporation are supposed to work as a tripartite. That's clearly laid out. We haven't had a workshop with all three of those entities in the [five years] I've been with the CDC."[97]

Subsequently, a new Urban Renewal Agency Board was formed with five citizen members and two City Councilors; the City Council became, once more, just a City Council. As one of the new Commissioners said, "It was time to refocus the Urban Renewal Agency's priorities, rebrand itself to the community and incentivize economic development."

Even with the changes, Ketchum's current Urban Renewal Board must deal with its problematic history. For one thing, the Starbucks site, purchased for affordable housing in 2010 for $3.2 million, was appraised at half that price in 2017, largely due to its lease agreement with Starbucks.[98] There may also be a shortfall in projected urban renewal income. It's possible that Ketchum will have financial problems when the urban renewal program sunsets and its debts come due, but those details are beyond the purview of this book.

Will a Diverse Economy Prevail?

As the Valley's small business owners pursue their passions and their dreams, they will inevitably push the economy forward. It is hard to stop entrepreneurs with an idea for a widget, a store, or a service that they think is better than what currently exists. Many of them will continue to make their mark for years. Others have already transferred their business to their kids. Still others will sell to another entrepreneur. And a few will fail. But all will benefit if Valley leaders and the small business community commit to building a diverse economy that nurtures entrepreneurial start-ups.

In 2018, Ketchum's Mayor held a "Fair on the Square" in which he asked people to dream about the City's future. Echoing surveys of previous years, people wanted more "live/work" spaces in the industrial area; affordable housing; a transportation hub; increased support for Main Street; more social and recreational activities for the younger set; and a more pedestrian friendly downtown. Written comments expressed the familiar desire to preserve the Valley's authenticity, livability, and quality of life. Today, there are a few more street entertainments in Ketchum, a proposed affordable housing project (although problematic for many due to its location and design), and a plan to preserve a few historic buildings. On the other hand, Ketchum is considering granting waivers to the Marriot Corporation for a proposed hotel at the City's entrance, waivers that would vastly increase the hotel's density, height, and footprint, and undermine Ketchum's small town character, contrary to the community's hopes. Nor has any initiative been proposed to support Main Street's development.

It has been 20 years since the Valley's first economic study, but we are no smarter and no further ahead with economic development planning. The tourist mantra prevails. Yet, today we hear more than ever of entrepreneurship's dominant role in the growth of the American economy. Magazines like *Inc.* (1969), *Entrepreneur* (1977), and *Fast Company* (1995) are entirely dedicated to profiling the clever creatives who have invented products and services of mind-boggling variety. National Public Radio's program, "How I Built This" and TV's "Shark Tank," dwell weekly on the struggles and successes of start-up founders, portraying them as role models of dogged entrepreneurship: persistent, willing to acknowledge mistakes, good-humored, and able to scrape together funding from seemingly impossible sources. Then, there is the on-going coverage of gutsy start-ups that have captured the country's imagination: Facebook, Spanx, Uber, Warby Parker, AirBnB, and Tesla, which Elon Musk describes as one part of his "collection of roughly a dozen technology startups which have nothing to do with traditional automotive companies."

Meanwhile, the Wood River Valley's small business community keeps chugging along, the backbone of our economy. The next chapter profiles 10 small business owners and their contributions to our lifestyle: the mom-and-pop shopkeepers who have served the community for years, the inventors, the corporate founders, the "don't tie me down" gig workers, and the self-employed people who, able to work anywhere, have chosen to live in our special Valley.

Chapter Seven

The Case for Entrepreneurs

Entrepreneurs and their small enterprises are responsible for almost all the economic growth in the United States.

—Ronald Reagan

Since early human history, people have created products and services to sell in local markets, to their neighbors, or to traders passing through. The need to provide for oneself and one's family is absolute, although people do it in different ways. Fast forward to the Wood River Valley in the 19ᵗʰ century: mountain men selling skins, miners selling ores, hot springs owners selling rooms, and ranchers selling sheep and cows. For roughly two centuries, this area's rich natural resources, rough beauty, and rustic, free-wheeling lifestyle have attracted risk-takers, eager to put their creative talents and skills to work in a new, unfettered environment.

Averell Harriman himself brought an entrepreneurial start-up to the Valley: the destination resort. Bill Janss and Earl Holding followed with their own entrepreneurial ideas to create an even more perfect vacation experience for the nation's and the world's visitors. Small businesses developed alongside the Resort, popping up in the towns, answering the needs of locals, bringing fresh ideas and opportunities into the economy. They wove the fabric of daily life, changing with the times to meet more contemporary needs and sometimes growing into big corporations. Today, Main Street offers sophisticated products and services typical of current times, helping to provide economic stability, an innovative culture, and circulating income.

Some local leaders have insisted that promoting entrepreneurship will harm the tourist economy, but how could it? Every tourist business was started by an entrepreneur. And who wouldn't want to visit or live in a thriving, innovative Valley that, along with great hotels, restaurants, and recreation, has clothing designers, technology specialists, artists, financial managers, consultants, inventors, and wellness professionals who provide a breadth and depth that is unique in an isolated, rural area?

The Role of Entrepreneurship

Nationally, statistics show that entrepreneurs have played a major role in generating new jobs and innovative ideas that continually refresh the economy. The numbers vary across research studies and from year to year, but the big picture is the same. Christina Romer, former Chair of the Council of Economic Advisers, has called small businesses the "engine of growth in the economy." On a national scale, small businesses supply the vast majority of new jobs each year and have a bigger economic impact than large corporations. According to the Small Business Administration, businesses with 1-500 employees comprise 99.9% of all U.S. firms and pay wages to 47.3% (nearly 60 million) of private sector employees. Businesses with fewer than 20 employees (typical of the Valley) tend to create the most jobs of all. They are even more likely to start in difficult circumstances: recessions, bear markets, and even Covid-19 epidemics.

Of course, not all start-ups endure: 20% of small businesses fail in their first year, 30% in their third year, 50% in their fifth year, and 70% by their tenth year. Jobs created by start-ups in any given year may be lost the next, lowering the numbers for "permanent" job creation. Nevertheless, even failed start-ups employ people for a year or two, and maybe more, often encouraging entrepreneurship in those they must let go. Further, since "once an entrepreneur, always an entrepreneur," someone who fails in the first or third or fifth year is likely to get right back at it again, often hiring past employees for their new business. In the long run, according to Forbes, a successful startup is more likely to turn $1 into $2, then $2 into $10, and $10 into $100 faster than an established corporation, and may well go on to become a familiar household name.

In the Valley and the nation, behind every tiny shop with just one or two employees, a large corporation, or a not-for-profit organization, there was a creative person with an idea or invention they thought would make a difference for others. Following their entrepreneurial instincts, they gathered funds, found a place to work, marketed their ideas and talents, and began to earn income. In starting something new, they were taking a risk, sometimes large, sometimes small. But each of them in the Wood River Valley has added jobs and earnings to the economy. It is to them that we owe much of our community well-being and comfortable lifestyle.

Check out the local entrepreneurial world yourself. Scan the phone book, look at the store fronts on Main Street, visit the second floor offices in commercial buildings and discover the number and range of previously unknown enterprises, the majority of which are not related to tourism. Talk with the owners and learn that most of their business income comes from a mix of locals, visitors, and second-home owners. A few, like art galleries and high-end clothing stores, sell primarily to short-term tourists; the rest estimate that their income mostly comes from locals and long-term second-home owners with just 20%-30% coming from short-term tourists.

Today, the Valley continues to attract entrepreneurs to its culture of personal independence and easy-going lifestyle. Here, they can pursue both a career and a quality lifestyle with a "work-life balance." In so doing, they reinforce the Valley's authenticity and values.

Entrepreneur Profiles

Between 2008 and 2011, I wrote 60 profiles for *The Weekly Sun* that described local start-ups, just a smidgeon of the Valley's small businesses. All of them have run their businesses for a decade or more and beaten the odds. Their stories are below: compelling, personal, and unique. They are your friends and supporters, colleagues and neighbors.

Nourish Me. Julie Johnson started out selling nutritional raw crackers made from seeds (a story in itself), aiming for national distribution. But she soon veered onto a wider track and opened a health food and supplement store, Nourish Me. Needing a loan, Johnson applied to the Ketchum Community Development Corporation but was turned down. Undeterred, she went to the USDA in Twin Falls and got the money she needed to open her store on Main Street in May 2010. She still sells her crackers (and ships them to customers around the country), but also offers organic seasonal produce, home-made healthy foods, a wide variety of supplements, and organic cosmetics to a health-oriented community. Julie is now certified in Nutritional Therapy and has focused on digestive problems that Nourish Me foods can help to alleviate. "The store was in the back of my mind for years," says Johnson. "As a child, I pulled my first carrot out of the rich, moist, dark soil of the Pacific Northwest and knew that good, clean food would be my life."

Rocky Mountain Hardware. Mark and Patsy Nickum's original business was selling custom windows and doors in Hailey. One day, an architect friend asked if they could create some bronze hardware for a client's home — hinges, doorstops, cabinet knobs — that would provide a unique interior theme. They did, and over time, the business shifted more and more to specialized hardware until, in 2002, the Nickum's son, Christian took over and dropped the line of windows and doors. Today, Rocky Mountain Hardware has a store on Ketchum's Main Street where it shows 24 lines of artisanal handmade architectural designs and helps feed the economy of two other Idaho towns. Blackfoot forges the hardware with Old-World casting techniques which are then etched and refined in Shoshone and finished and shipped out of Hailey to global clients. For Christian, "I grew up in the Valley and always wanted to come back. Fortunately, my parents had a business I could return to, one that enabled me to provide training and jobs for friends who also wanted to stay here."

Redfish Technology. With advancing communications technology, "location-neutral entrepreneurs" emerged in the late 1980s, able to work wherever they wanted, including the Valley. A good example is Rob Reeves who founded Redfish Technology when he was 25. The Hailey business recruits top professional and executive talent from around the country for positions in engineering, IT, sales, and marketing for America's high-tech companies. Reeves was headed for a banking career in Seattle, but then realized he wanted something different. When his brother told him about a recruiting job in the Valley, Rob came for an interview and was hired. Three years later he started Redfish Technology. He once contracted with remote workers in Rhode Island, Mexico, and Costa Rica, but has now chosen to operate strictly from his Hailey office. There he focuses on recruiting in niches with long-term potential: artificial intelligence, autonomous vehicles, health technology, and financial technology.

TATE Elbow System. Randy Acker, a veterinarian, is one of the better known business owners in the Valley as the founder of three local vet clinics. He is also an inventor, put to the task by his beloved yellow lab, Tate, known for balancing a pile of dog cookies on his nose for jaw-dropping lengths of time. When he was seven, however, Tate's elbows began to weaken. The usual treatments failed, and Acker asked a young local engineer, Greg Van Der Meulen, to help design an elbow implant. Van Der Meulen agreed and worked with Acker through the design and production of the implant's metal and plastic parts. Then, the pair patented the Tate Elbow Implant, a novel two-hour surgical "mill and drill" procedure, and the required instruments. The implant, now in its third evolution, is performed around the U.S. and in select European hospitals. Today, after a buyout and mergers, Greg is a location-neutral professional, based in Hailey as an employee of Movora, part of the Swedish company, Vimian.

Jennifer Diehl Production & Talent. Jennifer Diehl is a working mom who runs her business from home, producing photo shoots and commercials for lifestyle companies like Ariat, Brooks Running, Eddie Bauer, and Dooney & Burke. Diehl grew up in the Valley, a third generation local, but moved to Los Angeles after college to work in television production. "But commuting was not for me," she says. "Then my job went on hiatus and I needed to pay my rent!" So, she returned home and started modeling for a local talent agency. After the birth of her first baby boy, she bought the business. "I've broadened my scope and now do more production," she explains, adding, "There's no magic formula. I've provided dog sleds, truckloads of snow, yodeling skateboarders, and cows flown in by helicopter - whatever is needed for a seamless shoot." "But, best of all," she adds, "I can introduce people to a beautiful place that is my childhood, my livelihood, my parenthood," a place she knows will inspire her clients to be ambassadors for our precious Valley.

GameZoneGear LLC. Several local entrepreneurs manufacture products for sale in big box or specialty retail stores. A good example is Doug Niedrich and his son, Kyle, owners of GameZoneGear. Their patented "Drophats" include the QuikCamo camouflage cap for hunters (inspired by Doug's co-founder Nick Nichols) and sold at Walmart for four years as number one in its merchandise class. Made for one-handed operation, the basic cap is made of 3D leafy-covered camouflage material with a leafy mask (with eyeholes) that drops from the visor to conceal a hunter's face. The high-end version has eyeglass apertures, anti-fog capability, and screened ear and mouth holes. For Neidrich, a distinct advantage is "no more face paint" or having to quickly hide from a charging bull elk. QuikCamo has three major patterns, "Mossy Oak," "King's Camo," and "Realtree," as well as gloves and suits that allow hunters to disappear in their chosen terrain. Today, QuickCamo is sold through e-commerce companies and mom-and-pop stores nationwide.

Gail Severn Gallery. Soft-spoken and modest, Gail Severn has built one of the most successful art businesses in the community. Her 8,000 square foot space carries world-class contemporary art that can run into the high six figures. But it was not always this way. Severn came to the Valley 31 years ago for a job at Sun Valley Center for the Arts. The Director had forgotten her, however, and the job was gone. While tearfully sitting outside on the steps, a nice man asked what was wrong and offered her a job at Sun Valley Resort. The man was Bill Janss. A few weeks later, the Center found a job for her. In time, Severn started the Gail Severn Gallery in a tiny space, selling mugs and posters, the only items she could afford. Gradually, however, Severn expanded her business into what it is today, displaying the works of over 100 artists, publishing books and catalogues for her exhibitions, and participating in international art fairs. She credits lots of people for helping her make it happen, saying, "You can never do it alone. It should always be 'we', never 'me'!"

Sage School. Harry Weekes was an experienced teacher, trained in biology and adolescent brain development and learning when he started The Sage School, grades 6-12, in 2009. Today he has over 90 students. What prompted him? "It was the convergence of turning 40, being a mid-career professional with 20 years of experience, as well as trusting my abilities and my blossoming idealism," he says. Believing that adolescents have an emerging brain-based hunger to directly experience the world and learn from it, the school curriculum is based around human ecology with field trips, independent studies, and community action. Skills Block classes include math, Spanish, and writing. The Human Ecology block centers on multidisciplinary projects that blend science, the humanities, social science, history, the arts, and literature. Asked if he is an entrepreneur, Weekes laughs, "I lasted one day in college microeconomics, but I've had to be entrepreneurial to make the school a good product, market it, and be financially sound."

Eye Safety Systems (ESS). Much of the Valley's quality of life centers on outdoor recreation. A passionate kayaker, John Dondero's first business was Natural Progression Kayaks, started in 1973. "It wasn't sustainable, but it taught me about business, plastics, and product development," he says. Twenty-five years later, after designing ski goggles for Scott USA, Dondero founded Eye Safety Systems, plastic safety goggles that perform like sports eyewear but are incredibly sturdy. "I put everything on the line to get started. I had two kids in college, but I had made New Year's resolutions for four years to strike out on my own. I finally did it." California firefighters were his first sell. The Navy and the Army were more challenging but, eventually, they bought the goggles as well. Under Dondero's hand, ESS became the premier supplier of military eyewear in 100 countries. In 2007, ESS became a wholly-owned subsidiary of Oakley. Looking back, Dondero says, "It was the fulfillment of what anyone could dream for."

Wild Gift. Bob Jonas, born in Alaska and raised in the Wood River Valley, is an ardent spokesperson for the magic of wild lands.

He founded his first business, Sun Valley Trekking, a backcountry ski outfit, in 1982 and grew it to five overnight huts in the Wood River and Sawtooth Valleys. Twenty years later, after a two-year sabbatical to ski, dog sled, sea kayak, and backpack across Alaska, he sold the business to a young local couple. Then, he started a non-profit called "Wild Gift" to help "better world entrepreneurs." Each May, after a national search, Wild Gift selects five 21-30-year-olds committed to starting sustainability-driven organizations. They gather in the Valley for a 21-day trek across the Boulder-White Clouds Wilderness, sharing and refining their business plans with their colleagues and volunteer mentors before going back home to launch their enterprises. So far, Wild Gift has helped 75 fellows who work around the world in wildlands stewardship, sustainable agriculture, energy innovation, community development, affordable housing, and public policy.

The Entrepreneurial Mindset

The entrepreneurs profiled above chose to live in the Valley when they were young and exploring their next steps in life. They committed themselves to a rural lifestyle without necessarily knowing how they would earn a decent income. Then, they got an idea and, with tenacity, independence, and imagination, built a business or bought one and developed or revamped it according to their personal abilities and goals. Most had success with their first business and stayed with it. Others had a failure or two before moving on to create another start-up.

Despite their differences, they possessed the personality traits typical of entrepreneurs: confidence, adaptability, persistence, common sense, and a passionate idea about what they wanted in life. They relied on their intuition and took chances. Most started in modest circumstances — the garage, the kitchen, or a tiny office. Many had experience in their field before starting out and, as they moved ahead, reached out for mentoring, financing, connections, and general support. All are clever, creative, and open-minded.

Today, these 10 entrepreneurs are self-supporting. They provide income, jobs, and training for roughly 250 Valley residents. Each of them contributes to the community quietly with their time, products, and/or money. Their families sometimes work in the business but almost all serve in other community roles. Many of their children are following, or will follow, in their footsteps as entrepreneurs. It is these determined creatives who undergird a vibrant local culture and the Valley's everyday energy. They embody the features of a rugged valley that offers challenge and exploration to those with the guts to pursue them.

Five Strong Business Niches

Over the years, Valley entrepreneurs have built five strong business niches — pillars of local enterprise that continue to grow and generate new start-ups.

The first is food products. A pamphlet published by Community Supported Agriculture lists 40-plus local farms and ranches that supply fresh meat and vegetables, most of them organic, to local farmer's markets, restaurants, and grocery stores. Many sell prepared shelf products, including K&K Mountain Roast, KB Burritos, Ketchum Cookies, Lava Lake Lamb, Lyndees, Melt, Simple Kneads, Sun Valley Mustard, and Toni's Ice Cream. In a pet-loving town, Idahound's meats and treats for the family dog have been successful. Beverage companies include Rising Springs, Sawtooth Brewery, and Warfield Distillery. Bucksnort Root Beer started in the Valley but moved to Boise to expand (as has Melt). Earnings from this niche have yet to be measured.

A second niche, not surprisingly, is outdoor recreation products. Over the years, ESS, Scott USA, and Smith Goggles grew so effectively in the Valley that they were bought by conglomerates and have since moved on. But many remain and others have fledged here. They include clothing businesses: Club Ride Apparel, First Lite, Jutte, SQN Sport, and Vie Active; retail stores such as Backwoods, Elephant's Perch, Pete Lane's, and Sturtevant's; and outdoor guide businesses like Middle Fork River Expeditions, Silver Creek Outfitters, Sun Valley Heli-Skiing, and Sun Valley Trekking. Earnings from this niche have also yet to be measured.

For the many Valley aesthetes, the arts and humanities stand as a third pillar, comprised of five theater companies, 30 art galleries, two dance companies, talks by writers and historians, a local symphony, and at least ten signature events, including Trailing of the Sheep, Sun Valley Writers Conference, and Wagon Days. In 2016, this niche contributed $29.3 million to the Valley's earnings, provided 891 jobs, and made $2.1 million in tax payments to state and local governments. These figures do not include additional earnings by independent photographers, jewelry makers, videographers, ceramicists, and skilled craftsmen working in wood and metal. It is possible that the publicity generated by this niche attracts more income than any high-end hotel or tourist marketing, while also introducing vacationers to the Valley's vibrancy, authenticity, and scenic beauty.[99]

Philanthropy is a fourth major niche in the Valley, supported by several family foundations and philanthropic collectives like the Little Black Dress Club, 100 Men Who Care, and the Wood River Women's Charitable Foundation. Over 100 registered non-profit organizations address a wide range of community needs, including The Advocates, The Community Library, The Hunger Coalition, Mountain Humane, Sun Valley Museum of Art, and Wood River Hospice. According to the local Spur Foundation, this niche contributed $76 million in earnings to the Valley in 2018.

The Valley's fifth major niche revolves around health and wellness practitioners dedicated to serving our physical, mental and spiritual well-being, healing our bodies and minds: mental health professionals, naturopaths, personal fitness trainers, chiropractors, and reflexologists. Many sell manufactured and homemade health and wellness products through their offices, retail outlets, and farmer's markets. It is to them we owe the well-known, annual Sun Valley Wellness Festival and Conference, the longest running such conference in the world, with prominent speakers such as Deepak Chopra and Marianne Williamson. The earnings from this niche have not yet been measured.

The Virtues of Rural Life

For some, it might seem anomalous to promote entrepreneurship in an isolated rural Valley in the middle of Idaho. Aren't big cities the place to be for up-and-comers, given the wide span of job opportunities with potentially large financial rewards? But city life usually requires trade-offs: a stressful lifestyle, dirty air and water, traffic, and other personal assaults. Not everyone is willing to accept those sacrifices. Instead, interested in the quality of their everyday life, more and more people are choosing to live in small towns where they can start a business or work for a company located elsewhere. In Yellowstone, a survey found that, even if businesses there could be more profitable in an urban setting, 86% would stay in Yellowstone. A 2020 Gallup poll reported that 48% of Americans would prefer to live in a small town or rural area, up from 39% in 2018.[100] This taste for a more rural life may explain why two keynote speakers at Sun Valley Economic Development's 2018 conference advised the Valley to stop defining itself as a tourist/resort area and brand itself as a place that offers calm, peace, and community.

Martin Zwilling, founder of Startup Professionals, an on-line consulting group, advocates small towns as better places to start successful businesses than what he calls "sacred hubs" like Silicon Valley, applauding them for their "healthy dose of localized flavor."[101] Scott USA, ESS, and Smith Goggles were local start-ups. When they were bought by large corporations with distant headquarters, their employees had to choose between staying behind or leaving a beloved Valley. It was a difficult choice for many. Power Engineers, which started in Hailey, still has its headquarters there but has established multiple offices around the world. Marketron is also headquartered in the Valley but operates offices in Opelika, Alabama, and Denver, Colorado.

Many rural areas have become aware of how attractive they are to city-dwellers and are developing local entrepreneurship to revive, and sustain, their economies. Examples are Wytheville, Virginia (population 8,000); Sikeston Missouri (16,000); Aberdeen, South Dakota (28,000); and Redmond, Oregon (30,000).[102] They hope, much as many families in our Valley do, that "boomerang" kids who grew up in their towns, and then moved to the city for college or a job, will want to move back to the low-key atmosphere of their youth.

Some people choose never to leave their hometown. Jason Duff, award-winning founder and CEO of COMSTOR Outdoor in Huntsville, Ohio recently told *Inc.* Magazine that he had rejected the "hype" of Silicon Valley, choosing instead to build "'old fashioned, profitable, multimillion-dollar businesses (that created) hundreds of jobs in my community." He achieved his dream before he was 30 and still lives in Huntsville, population 523 in 2019.[103]

Chapter Eight

The Future Is Now!

*There is no power for change greater than a community
discovering what it cares about."*

—Meg Wheatley

It is time to plan for the Valley's future — now — before it's too late
and we lose the community and lifestyle that we love so much. In
previous chapters, we've looked back at our history, the three entrepreneurs who built an outstanding Resort, and the Valley that grew
up around it. We know that local leaders have pursued tourism as the
major source of income since the early days, despite conclusions from
experts that the economy needs diversification to remain durable, stable, and healthy. We know there is a core of entrepreneurs who have
always anchored the economy and continue to do so in different ways.
Finally, we know that small towns across America are re-defining
themselves as entrepreneurial communities, eager to build talent and
businesses from within.

But there is no long-term economic plan for the Wood River Valley. As Yogi Berra once said in his special wisdom, "If you don't know where you are going, you'll end up someplace else." That describes our current situation. Asked what the Valley will be like in 10 years, most residents hesitate, shrug their shoulders, and say, "I just don't know. It's hard to predict, isn't it?" Some want to turn the clock back thirty years. Others fear becoming a commercialized, crowded tourist town. Still others praise the Valley's protected high-end life, attracting "the top levels of society while remaining uncrowded, low-key, quiet, and private."

We have been lucky. Sun Valley Resort was the right business at the right time for the Wood River Valley, built by a benevolent business owner who was fair and responsive to the community. Averell Harriman gave the Valley a unique economic anchor and Steve Hannigan marketed it to America with panache, publicity, and purpose. Together, they put the Wood River Valley on the map and the Resort became an industry leader in its time.

As Bill Janss and Earl Holding worked further wonders with the Resort, the Valley synthesized its own personal style and reputation. The economy expanded to meet the needs of increasingly sophisticated East Coast, West Coast and Midlands Americans, and a culture emerged that valued creativity, education, health care, business skills, the arts, sustainability, respect for others, and a casual atmosphere. In many ways, the "Valley of the Sun" became the "Valley of Opportunity."

And it still is. Today, our community is praised for its expressive and freedom-loving lifestyle. In service to that lifestyle, will must build a more diverse entrepreneurial culture that keeps our economy healthy, growing, and strong. Can we do even more than other small towns are doing across America? Can we go so far as to lead our industry again by building entrepreneurship into the Valley's identity? If so, we might add another chapter to our history of invention, lay a path for other destination resorts to follow.

I believe we can do these things if we want to. Below are draft strategic planning steps that we can easily plan to take together in the near future.

Establish Leadership

First, we need an organized group of strong, informed, and independent business leaders who agree on the need for a healthier, more diverse economy. Since previous organizations have failed at this, does it make sense to create yet another? Yes, it does. But it must have certain, previously missing, elements. Group members must share an affinity for economic development in its broad sense. Some background experience in planning would help. The group must remain separate from, but able to collaborate with and learn from local and regional governments and agencies. It must seek and respectfully respond to public input. It must rely on hard evidence to back its decisions. Finally, while the leaders work pro bono, it must have a small paid staff and volunteers to conduct operations.

The right people are out there, yet unidentified, but necessary. In *Our Towns: A 100,000 Mile Journey Into the Heart of America,* James and Deborah Fallows observed that towns that thrived after the 2008 Recession did so because they had leaders who stepped forward with big-picture, long-term community goals, and were able to draw locals together around those goals.[104]

The *Idaho Mountain Express* agrees that active support for the business community is lacking. In an October 2019 editorial, the paper urged North Valley businesses to re-form a Chamber of Commerce, writing, "Today, no one explains the challenges in local business to government officials and administrators, many of whom have never operated a business. A vacuum exists...that punishes local businesses and their employees and lets the strong voices of people with little or no connection to the local economy prevail."[105]

The *Express* is right. Whether or not a new Chamber is the solution, the Valley needs an organization of some sort to provide business services, help build increased economic diversity, support start-ups, and pursue a feasible economic development plan. Such an organization might be called "Business Trailblazers," leading the Valley into the future.

An outstanding role model for Business Trailblazers would be Silicon Valley Couloir in Jackson, Wyoming.[106] Its mission — "to align entrepreneurship with community vision to promote a diverse economy and a healthy environment for current and future generations" — says it all. The Couloir has successfully promoted entrepreneurship for 14 years in the Teton Valley region with programs for both start-ups and experienced business owners, including introductions to accredited investors, monthly networking events with panel discussions and speed networking, coworking space with office amenities, and annual pitch days for cash prizes.

A local Business Trailblazers could undertake other efforts as well. It could raise a revolving loan fund for start-ups from investors (local and otherwise) and government sources. It could hire a lobbyist to press for local and state government decisions that advance small business interests. It might work with the Valley's school system to write a curriculum that fosters next generation creatives. (A few years ago, two local elementary school kids created products picked up by Nike and Home Depot. The parents, not knowing how to make deals, signed away the rights to the inventions).

Another source of help for Trailblazers would be the National Center for Economic Gardening.[107] Conceived in an economically depressed Littleton, Colorado in 1987, it has created the oldest and best tested entrepreneurial development program in the United States, helping towns to "grow" Main Street from within, rather than trying to persuade outside businesses to relocate. Since its inception, the Center has worked with roughly 3,500 towns to develop entrepreneurial economies, using advanced technologies to ensure success.

Finally, the Small Business Administration (SBA), already serving the Valley, could provide help. An advocate for Main Street in general, and economic gardening in specific, the SBA believes that "Just like growing plants and vegetables for a garden, growing entrepreneurs and creating jobs increase the vibrancy of your town. Both are essential nutrients for economic development and sustainability." Working with Trailblazers, the SBA could provide counselors to help startups explore and refine their ideas, develop business plans, and connect with funding sources.[108]

Additional information and networking resources include regional and national organizations that advocate for entrepreneurship; business school gurus; other small towns that are building an entrepreneurial culture; and programs such as Goldman Sachs' 10,000 Small Businesses Initiative which provides education, investment capital, and support services to entrepreneurs.[109]

Define the Mission

Having organized around a general purpose, Business Trailblazers must articulate a vision and a mission that will drive its efforts, brainstorming these on its own and then seeking public tweaking and agreement.

Thirty years ago, a County Commissioner, looking ahead to the Valley's growth, stated, "Preservation of the past and protection of the future are the twin horns of the dilemma," but the dilemma was never resolved. Our past has been marked by originality, authenticity, and a Western aura; our future can be designed to protect these elements. In line with the Commissioner's thoughts, one possible vision might be: "We are committed to preserving our community's historic past as we build an historic future." The mission might be: "We will create

an entrepreneurial culture that honors our past, present, and future."
(These suggestions are offered as examples to help stimulate thinking,
not as "the answers.")

Sun Valley Resort might benefit from the effort as well since it
is also struggling with how to preserve the past yet anticipate the
future. In a New York Times interview, an advertising executive for
the Resort described it as, "one of the more difficult marketing challenges… (with) 'top-of-the line facilities and Mayberry…The place
needs to be introduced to a new generation… (but) if you invite the
wrong people…they'll change it, and they'll ruin it."[110] A Resort
executive agreed, saying "(T)he Resort has "a unique beauty (that's)
not for everyone…The good news and the bad news is that it's a very
special place…yet (to) still make it relevant to another generation is
the challenge…."

Tim Egan, an author who knows our community well, would encourage us to find and celebrate what he calls a "shared narrative:" the histories, stories, and myths we have woven together, intertwining strands
from the past and the present that will echo into the future as well.

Draft an Economic Development Strategy

Once Business Trailblazers has formed and sketched out a compelling vision and mission, it will be important to get the public's help in
designing a strategic plan. This is best done with focus groups (facilitated meetings of 8-10 people from the community's different seg-
ments), followed by a community-wide survey, to identify where the
Valley is, wants to go, and how it will get there. Questions should dig
into the Valley's strengths and weaknesses, the economy's strengths
and weaknesses, what people would like to see in the future, the roles
that entrepreneurship and tourism play in the Valley, and why or why
not creating a more diverse economy is a good idea.

Then, Business Trailblazers must gather data about Main Street:
the number of businesses, their niches and subniches, the type and

number of jobs they offer, their contributions to the Valley's earnings, their growth strategies for the next two-three years, and the resources they would find most helpful. It would also be good for the organization to learn how other entrepreneurial towns are strategizing about economic development.

With this information, Trailblazers should be able to formulate an economic development strategy and goals for the Valley in about 12 months, including priorities, tasks, timelines, and accountabilities. It will also need to create a budget and pursue funding from Valley governments, local and regional investors, government and institutional grants, public/private partnerships, and business memberships. Finally, once the economic development strategy is implemented, it will need periodic monitoring to ensure it's on track toward its goals.

With the right people and marketing, Trailblazer's work will energize public interest, participation, and enthusiasm. Newcomers might become more aware of our values and get involved. As Margaret Mead once said, "Never underestimate the power of a small group of committed people to change the world. In fact, it is the only thing that ever has."

Synthesize a Brand

During the focus group process, a few minutes should be spent on brainstorming the Valley's identity, or "brand." Brands and their taglines are important. Coca Cola sells "The original great taste;" Nike encourages "Just do it;" and Duracell's Energizer Bunny "Just keeps going and going and going...." The identity of these well-known companies has long been established, but their campaigns remind us with phrases (sometimes called tag lines) that are memorable, durable, consistent (despite variations on a theme), and distinguish each company's products from its competitors.[111] As a general theme, the Valley's brand today is quality of life. The elements that represent it are uniqueness, a Western aura, healthy outdoor living, real, authentic, family-friendly, down-to-earth, welcoming, rural, and yet sophisticated. To these we can potentially add creative, entrepreneurial, and economically vibrant. The final task for Business Trailblazers would be to pull these elements together into an evocative phrase that captures the essence of the Valley and promotes it, a phrase that works well with the chosen vision and mission.

At one point, the Valley had an excellent marketing campaign with the tag line "Small Town, Big Life," portrayed in a dynamic video that focused entirely on the Valley's strengths as a business base, characterizing our community as "breaking the mold" and a place for "world class businesses." Entrepreneurs were profiled who first moved to the Valley for its rich outdoor life and friendly community before starting successful businesses. The film never once mentions tourism. Perhaps that's why the marketing campaign was barely promoted. Today, Ketchum has, unfortunately, snagged the words "Small Town, Big Life" for its website home page (omitting the video), emphasizing only tourist interests and making no reference to our vibrant business community. You can find the video on Vimeo.[112]

Preserving Our Quality of Life

Economic development, as we have discussed, goes beyond growth numbers to encompass all aspects of a community's quality of life. Three issues in addition to building an entrepreneurial economy are especially important: living sustainably, preparing for climate change, and managing population growth. Each of them, highlighted below, must be addressed in an economic development strategy.

Sustainability and climate change are closely linked. We must live sustainably in the face of climate change, trying to slow it down by protecting the resources and biological processes that the natural world (including humans) needs to survive. Fortunately, the Valley values sustainability. Maintaining open space through land trusts, conservation easements, and codified limitations on land development has been a priority for years. Local agriculturalists practice organic crop and animal farming and sell their products through a regional market network. New construction increasingly fulfills LEED certification requirements. Solar energy has become more prominent in home construction. The use of electric energy for cars and buses is on the rise.

We have an excellent resource in The Sun Valley Institute for Resilience, an anchor and advocate for many of these efforts.[113] We also have the Climate Action Coalition of Wood River Valley formed in 2020 to gain Valley-wide commitment to 100% clean electric sources by 2035 and 100% clean energy by 2045. Four out of five local governments (Blaine County, Ketchum, Hailey and Bellevue) have signed the pact and the City of Sun Valley is considering the idea.[114] But we can still do more, and must, considering that our home state of Idaho has little regard for conservation.[115]

Of major importance, Sun Valley Resort began several years ago to pursue conservation practices, moving beyond its previous indifference to environmental protection. In 2013-2014 it received in "A" for protecting watersheds and habitat. It has installed energy-efficient snow guns and a recycling/composting program. New construction and retro-fits are more energy efficient.[116] The Resort has pledged to be a steward of the environment.[117] Additional conservation methods, already in practice at other ski areas around the country, may be on the docket for implementation. We can hope so because they will be needed to protect the Resort's business viability, given the ongoing impact of global warming on the ski industry: inevitably warmer temperatures, wetter snow and less of it, shorter ski seasons, a decline in industry income, and abandoned low-altitude resorts.

Population growth is a third critical factor that will affect our future. In 1998, Blaine County's buildout capacity was 80,000 people, four times today's population contained in the same narrow glacial trough.[118] A County Commissioner at the time believed that peak population capacity was closer to 50,000 due to eventual water limits. Still, that is 2.5 times larger than our current population, and water rights are already a bone of contention for several constituencies, especially given the recent extended drought.

Although population levels have held steady for several years, the Valley recently experienced a lightning-fast expansion of roughly 1,500 residents after the appearance of the Covid-19 virus. Even when Covid ends, the trend to leave cities for rural areas will continue. Locally, school enrollment has soared; growth has exceeded that of the last seven years, and we will soon be pressed for more educational capacity and services. As our population ages (the median age is 54-61 and the 65-plus demographic has grown 140% since 2000), our health care system will need upgrades and adjunct care providers.[119] An economic development plan needs to anticipate these changes and provide workable solutions.

Simultaneous with the Valley's population growth, the number of available blue- and white-collar workers has diminished due to the lack of sufficient and decent affordable housing. Local governments have offered last-minute solutions: tent cities and permission for recreation vehicles to house Valley employees on private property. Meanwhile, more long-term and logical possibilities have yet to be pursued: issuing municipal bonds, altering zoning regulations, creating a charitable housing trust, forming public/private partnerships, and building on empty sites already designated for affordable housing. The crisis has deeply affected the Main Street community. Some businesses have postponed expansion; others have cut back on their services and hours, including the Resort. A few have shut their doors. Others may soon follow.

Fortunately, some of the community's critical needs will provide opportunities for savvy entrepreneurs, both locals and newcomers. New businesses and new business ideas will emerge as they often do in crises. And, if the Valley develops a more diverse entrepreneurial culture, we will be able to provide better paying jobs and career opportunities than the tourist industry has ever provided.

The Mystique Still Exists

Dorice Taylor, the woman who loved the Wood River Valley and so successfully publicized the Resort during the Harriman years, wrote the following in her 1980 book, *Sun Valley.* "A young woman coming to the Valley today won't see the quaint little village I saw (in 1938). But there will be no high-rises; there will be snow on the roofs and the sky will be blue. In this sun-drenched world she will feel the mystique of the Valley just as I did some forty years ago and say, 'This is it. Somehow, some way, I am going to get back here to stay."

Would Taylor, visiting the Valley today, repeat those sentiments? How would she feel about the multi-story brick banks and six-story hotel on Ketchum's Main Street? Would she miss the intimate warmth of the Duchin Room? Would she wonder where the ski bums and their hangouts are? Maybe. Maybe not. But, if brought up to date about today's tourist economy — the commercial conformity, large crowds, and vulnerability to environmental catastrophes — she might, as a businesswoman, agree that pursuing tourism alone is not wise. What worked well in one era is hardly likely to work in another.

But she would probably still feel the palpable charm and mystique of our close-knit community living quietly in an historic, lovely, and protected mountain setting. She might even catch a whiff of the "geezerdom" that Tim Egan referred to. After all, the mystique and geezerdom still linger, suffused through the community's collective memory, history, traditions, and habits of daily life. They are the reason why those who moved to the Valley thirty years ago — or just last week — want to close the doors behind them: to preserve the special community character they fell in love with.

So, while elements of the Valley's mystique are steadily being diluted, enough of an authentic atmosphere remains to be nourished and preserved. To avoid the regrets of those who cherish it, the community must make a concerted effort to retain that special mystique. The Valley is full of parents and grandparents who hope their children and grandchildren will return to create their own businesses and raise families. A good many of them are already here. Others are gaining experiences elsewhere before coming back. We need to guarantee they will be welcomed by a vibrant, innovative business community in which they can find their place.

The legendary photographer of the American West, David Stoecklein, once praised the Wood River Valley saying, "There's no place like it left in America." Known for his outgoing nature and devotion to the West, would Stoecklein be cheering us on, wherever he is, to preserve the distinct aura and heritage of our beloved Valley? Would he urge each of us who truly values the Valley's special way of life to devote ourselves to a shared community vision, a clear set of future-oriented goals, and an evocative brand that includes economic diversity and entrepreneurship? Would he read this book as a tombstone marking the Valley's past, or see it as the path toward a prized future?

I began this book describing Pale Rider, the classic Clint Eastwood movie in which "Preacher" saves a small community of placer miners from an encroaching hydraulic mining firm. Guided by a solid economic development plan for a diverse, entrepreneurial economy, Preacher's moral might today be reframed as "A small community of independent business owners pursuing their dreams is preferable to relying on one dominant business or industry. In the long run, a virtuous, economically diverse, and self-sufficient community is simply better for the land and the well-being of its people."

It would be nice if Preacher rode out of the Boulder Mountains tomorrow to save the Wood River Valley from a scenario it might regret. But preserving our Valley's heritage and charm will happen only if the Valley's leaders and residents take the steps to make it happen, rather than just hoping or wishing for it. Only a unified community will be able to do it, working to fulfill a common vision, and pursuing the right kind of economic development plan to get there.

The future is now! Let's get going in honor of Averell Harriman, Bill Janss, and Earl Holding, distinguished men and accomplished entrepreneurs who laid the groundwork for the Valley to evolve into the inspiring, beloved, and unique community that it is today! Let's not let them down!

Acknowledgements

I have very patient friends for whom I am eternally grateful. They encouraged, flattered, cheered, pushed, and coached me as I brought this book to fruition. Indeed, it was an unexpected journey, personal and professional, over parts of five years, and my friends hung with me all the way.

Readers with great questions, corrections, and encouragement in the earlier stages include Sue Bailey, Len Harlig, Charlie Hunt, Sally McCollum, Mike Medberry, Janet Schaumberg, and Ellery Sedgewick. Danielle Travers came back to town toward the end and greatly enriched the last chapter.

Many people who provided content for the book shall remain anonymous, but I thank them deeply as well.

Narda Pitkethly and Doris Moress lit my determination when it flagged with their laughter, empathy, advice, and understanding during moments of struggle and uncertainty. Pat Duggan was ever-present with all the above, plus her words of wisdom.

Ed Grant, eternal author, sympathized with me about the writing process, and spontaneously recited quotes about the craft from Hemingway. Bob Jonas, another eternal author, gave me the sense that it was okay to take my time and work out my thoughts.

Heidi Dalzell-Finger was my rock, reading, reading again, rereading after that, always genuinely interested, and always helpful with trenchant questions and excitement about my progress.

And, of course, there is the Ketchum Community Library, that bastion of books, services, and graciously helpful people, especially

Buffy. You all are a monument to knowledge, the power of books and media to draw people together, and the importance of continued learning and growth.

I am so thankful that I have been able to rely on you all and that you took the time to help me write this book. You were my guiding lights as I made the slow march forward. Bless you all!

The Local Impact of Covid-19

I was finishing this book when the first case of Covid-19 struck Blaine County on March 14, 2019 with community spread evident less than a week later. We soon became a national hotspot. Then, case numbers dropped until the holiday season drew visitors from November 2019 through January 2020 when they rose again. They have risen and fallen since even as most Valley residents and visitors have followed masking guidelines throughout the crisis. As of this writing in early September 2021, 65% of the local population has been fully vaccinated. Schools have reopened. Since the onset of the pandemic, *The New York Times* reports 2,627 reported cases of Covid-19 in Blaine County and 21 deaths.

While the Valley's hot spot status made the front page of *The New York Times*, it didn't deter an influx of new residents escaping California, Washington, and other states across the country, an influx that has created tensions between the "old-timers" and the "newbies" unfamiliar with Valley ways. Locals typically welcome new people, but we have had to make a conscious effort to demonstrate and sustain our values while educating fledgling residents about the Valley's lifestyle. A large colorful banner hanging from the fence along a major thoroughfare reads, "Don't Change Sun Valley. Let Sun Valley Change You."

Real estate prices have soared. Housing stock is virtually impossible to find. Undeveloped land has nearly doubled in price. New homes are going up everywhere. One resident, selling a modest home last June for $1.2 million on a side street in Ketchum, had 13 offers and finally agreed to sell for $1.8 million. That may, or may not, be one of the more extreme examples.

Meanwhile, the *Idaho Mountain Express* reported this past winter that, "Despite the trials of 2020, most businesses…are welcoming customers in 2021.[1] And, for all the difficulties, some are doing very well," especially those that implemented methods to keep customers safe (such as meal take-out and curbside pickup). A few believe their business is more efficient than ever, although this is partly due to not having enough employees, as has happened across the country.

Today, the Valley is in a "wait-and-see" mode, providing regular updates and imposing restrictions when the ebb and flow of the virus make it necessary. Fortunately, we are all working well together with mutual respect and concern.

---

[1] **welcoming customers in 2021:** Greg Foley. "For some Ketchum businesses, there's a silver lining in the Covid cloud." *Idaho Mountain Express.* March 24, 2021. bit.ly/3uCDMXt.

Endnotes

Introduction: The Big Picture

1. **simply better for the land:** Paul Smith. *Clint Eastwood: A Cultural Production.* (Minneapolis, Minnesota: University of Minnesota Press, 1993).

2. **many became ghost towns:** Joel Reichenberger. "Author maps the way to 36 abandoned ski resorts." *Steamboat Pilot & Today.* December 7, 2008. www.steamboatpilot.com/explore-steamboat/author-maps-the-way-to-36-abandoned-ski-resorts/.

3. **reshaped or vastly diluted:** Clifford, Hall. *Downhill Slide: Why the Corporate Ski Industry is Bad for Skiing, Ski Towns, and the Environment.* (San Francisco, California: Sierra Club Books, 2002).

One: Before Fame and Fortune

4. **Chapter One:** Many thanks to the authors whose books provided much of my background information: Wendolyn Holland, *Sun Valley: An Extraordinary History* (1998), and Doug Oppenheimer, *Sun Valley* (1976). (See Bibliography).

5. **Village in the City of Sun Valley:** Tony Tekaroniake Evans. "In Mining Era, Natives Clung to Traditions." *Idaho Mountain Express.* April 6, 2011. archives.mtexpress.com/index2.php?ID=2005136017.

6. **the unborn of the future nation:** The Constitution of the Iroquois Nation. www.indigenouspeople.net/iroqcon.htm.

7. **their remnants are still visible:** The provisions of the 1872 Mining Law are still in force. Today, there are an estimated 2,582 acres of public land patented for mining in Blaine County. Patents cost $2.50-$5.00 and there are no royalties for ores obtained by domestic or foreign companies. See David Gerard's "The Mining Law of 1872: Digging A Little Deeper." *PERC.* December 1, 1997. www.perc.org/1997/12/01/the-mining-law-of-1872-digging-a-little-deeper/.

8. **Mining and Smelting Company:** For a wealth of information on mining see John Lundin, especially his "Philadelphia Smelter: Processing Facility for Wood River Valley's Silver." *Presentation to The Community Library in Ketchum.* June 30, 2015. bit.ly/3dFWUOa.

9. **inform the several thousand residents:** The Library of Congress reports four newspapers in the Wood River Valley in the 1880s: *Hailey's Wood River Times* (1882-1915); *Bellevue's Wood River News* (1881-1882); *Hailey's Wood River Miner* (1881-1882); and the *Ketchum Keystone* (1883-1889).

10. **spirited, innovative, and inspired:** Roderick Frazier Nash. *Wilderness and the American Mind (Fourth edition).* (New Haven: Yale University Press, 1982).

11. **Native Americans and buffalo:** John Gast. American Progress, 1872. *Picturing United States History.* picturinghistory. gc.cuny.edu/john-gast-american-progress-1872/.

12. **parlors and music rooms:** Florence Blanchard. "Hot Springs Hotels of the Wood River Valley." *Sun Valley Magazine.* October 5, 2010. sunvalleymag.com/articles/hot-springs-hotels/. Also see John Lundin's slide show "Wood River Valley's Resort Hotels Before Sun Valley." Ketchum Community Library, June 23, 2015. www.slideshare.net/

CommunityLibrary/wood-river-valleys-hot-springs-resorts-by-john-lundin-2015?next_slideshow=1.

Two: Wise Visionary – W. Averell Harriman

13. **Chapter Two:** Again, many thanks to the following authors for their comprehensive background information: Rudy Abramson, Spanning the Century (1992); Wendolyn Holland, *Sun Valley: An Extraordinary History*, (1998); Walter Isaacson and Jim Thomas, *The Wise Men* (1986); Doug Oppenheimer, *Sun Valley* (1976). (See Bibliography).

14. **The ranch is now a public park:** More information on Railroad Ranch can be found at Island Park Reservations. islandparkidaho.com/history/harriman.html.

15. **not too wet or too much of it:** Jennifer Tuohy. "The Count of Sun Valley." *Sun Valley Guide.* Winter 2011-2012. www.svguide.com/w12/count.php. (The article has a nice overview of correspondence between Schaffgotsch and Harriman).

16. **bathing girls into the paper:** "Steve Hannigan's Girls." *Life Magazine.* November 30, 1936. bit.ly/3Cq91t121.

17. **magazine's most noted photographers:** "East Goes West to Sun Valley, Society's Newest Winter Playground." *Life Magazine.* Photos by Eisenstadt. March 8, 1037. bit.ly/3Cbp1im.

18. **slats strapped to their feet:** Karen Bossick. "Rustic Jewels." *Sun Valley.com.* December 31, 2008. sunvalleymag.com/articles/rustic-jewels/.

19. **recreation in a restful place:** James Varley. "Sun Valley's War: Home for wounded vets came to aid of struggling resort town." *MagicValley.com.* August 21, 2011. magicvalley.com/news/opinion/sun-valleys-war-home-for-wounded-vets-came-to-aid-of-struggling-resort-town/article_57e0a612-11ad-50db-bafc-f1ddbc27729e.html.

20. **tells wonderful tales:** Dorice Taylor. *Sun Valley.* Ex Libris: Sun Valley, Idaho, 1980.

21. **such a short period of time:** For a wonderful, concise history of Harriman's business and political life, see Alan Oser's article, "Ex-Governor Averell Harriman, Adviser to 4 presidents Dies." *The New York Times.* July 27, 1986. nyti. ms/3zIkyC1.

Three: Benevolent Ski Enthusiast – Bill Janss

22. **Chapter Three:** As in earlier chapters, I drew on other authors for background information and greatly appreciate their work: Wendolyn Holland, *Sun Valley: An Extraordinary History* (1998) and Doug Oppenheimer, *Sun Valley* (1976). (See Bibliography). Bob Ottum's, "Into the Valley of Fun" in *Sports Illustrated,* January 4, 1965, was also helpful. vault.si.com/vault/1965/01/04/into-the-valley-of-fun.

23. **"the Janss Dynasty":** Sam Enriquez. "A Family Fortune." *Los Angeles Times.* January 4, 1987. articles.latimes.com/1987-01-04/local/me-1949_1_family-business.

24. **protested the Vietnam War:** Susan Heller Anderson. "Edwin Janss, 74, A Developer of Suburbs and Two Ski Resorts." *Obituaries.* March 18, 1989. nyti.ms/39DJG24.

25. **feed our own animals:** Mike Riedel and Gretchen Guard. "Interview with Bill Janss." *Ketchum Community Library.* January 1, 1983. Much of the information and most of Janss' quotes in this chapter came from this interview; it gives a great sense of who Janss was.

26. **a community's connection to nature:** L.A. Times Archives. "Bill Janss Sr. Helped Establish Thousand Oaks." *Los Angeles Times.* December 7, 1996. www.latimes.com/archives/la-xpm-1996-12-07-me-6564-story.html.

27. **changed the industry's face:** Richard White and John M. Findley (eds). *Power and Place in the North American West.* (Seattle, Washington: University of Washington Press, 1999).

28. **blind turn to slow you down:** "Where to Ski Now." *Men's Journal.* October 13, 2018. www.mensjournal.com/travel/where-to-ski-now-20131018/.

29. **deficits under Union Pacific:** "Harry Holmes, 1925-2014." *San Francisco Chronicles Obituaries.* November 7, 2014-November 14, 2014. legcy.co/3zpZMYX.

30. **Love This Skiing Village:** Horace Sutton. "Wizard of Oz Would Love This Ski Village." *The Lakeland Ledger.* February 3, 1974. *bit.ly/3gB04n4*

31. **four more corporate owners:** Lucien Rhodes. "Kuolt's Complex." *Inc.* April 1, 1986. www.inc.com/magazine/19860401/4548.html. This is a fascinating profile of the founder of Horizon Air (an Elkhorn owner) and his struggles with leadership.

32. **arts advocate for the Valley:** Kate Algee. "A Spark that Started a Fire: The Artistic Revolution of Sun Valley." *Sun Valley Magazine.* December 11, 2013. bit.ly/3pRzBWE.

33. **rock, classical, and folk concerts:** Tony Tekaroniake Evans. "The Soul of a Community: Glenn Janss on the how the SVMoA got its start." *Idaho Mountain Express.* June 23, 2021. www.mtexpress.com/arts_and_events/events/the-soul-of-a-community-glenn-janss-on-the-how-the-svmoa-got-its-start/article_de89993e-d3a9-11eb-9063-d7e7d6730795.html. This is an excellent, informative interview with Janss.

34. **earnings of nearly $3,000,000:** Americans for the Arts. "Arts and Economic Prosperity 5 – Wood River Valley." www.americansforthearts.org/sites/default/files/aep5/PDF_Files/PRINTABLE_FindingsForAllStudyRegions.pdf.

35. **Silver Creek Preserve:** Brant Oswald. "Idaho's Silver Creek." www.brantoswaldflyfishing.com/articles.php?s=idahos-silver-creek.

36. **conservation efforts ever undertaken:** Silver Creek Preserve. *The Nature Conservancy.* 2020. www.nature.org/en-us/get-involved/how-to-help/places-we-protect/silver-creek-preserve/.

Four: Supreme Control – Earl Holding

37. **business in the United States:** Guy Boulton. "Earl Holding: Maverick Entrepreneur has made a fortune through hard work and patience." *Salt Lake Tribune.* April 20, 2013. archive.sltrib.com/article.php?id=56191172&itype=cmsid. Boulton's article was a rich source of information and quotes for this chapter.

38. **management at the Resort:** Mountain Express Editorial. "Speak Up, Earl." *Idaho Mountain Express.* 1977.

39. **a four-letter word:** Greg Foley. "The Valley pays tribute to Earl and Carol Holding." *Idaho Mountain Express.* January 25, 2006. archives.mtexpress.com/index2.php?ID=2005107587. This retrospective of Holding's life provided much background information for this chapter.

40. **terms other than money:** Mountain Express Editorial. "The Continued Inability of the Press." *Idaho Mountain Express.* April 4, 1977.

41. **than in the Gulf Coast:** Luisa Kroll. "Remembering Robert Earl Holding, Billionaire Owner of Sun Valley Ski Resort." *Forbes.* April 22, 2013. bit.ly/3cGlka0. This is another article with rich background on Holding's success and several quotes used in this chapter.

42. **he had and so he did:** Sports Illustrated Staff. "Earl has bought a pearl." *Sports Illustrated*. November 14, 1977. vault. si.com/vault/1977/11/14/earl-has-bought-a-pearl.

43. **black and blue from falling:** Andrew Slough. "Interview with Earl and Carol Holding." *Men's Adventure Travel.* Reprint in 2021. mensadventuretravel.com/adventure/idaho-earl-holding-interview. A lively article with good information and quotes.

44. **group's efforts failed, however:** Sports Illustrated Staff. *Scorecard.* September 11, 1978. vault.si.com/vault/1978/09/11/scorecard.

45. **$23 million on snowmaking:** Andrew Slough. "Interview with Earl and Carol Holding." *Men's Adventure Travel.* Reprint in 2021. mensadventuretravel.com/adventure/idaho-earl-holding-interview.

46. **ski destination unlike any other:** Larry Olmsted. "World's Best Ski Resorts: Sun Valley, Idaho" Forbes. February 22, 2016. www.forbes.com/sites/larryolmsted/2016/02/22/worlds-best-ski-resorts-sun-valley-idaho/2/.

47. **skier numbers no longer seem to matter:** "Where to Ski Now." *Men's Journal.* www.mensjournal.com/travel/where-to-ski-now-20131018/big-sky-mt/.

48. **in return for cultural exposure:** Angelo Young. "J-1 Visa Abuse: Employers Exploit Foreign Students Under US Government Program Meant for Cultural Exchange." *International Business Times.* December 9, 2015. www.ibtimes.com/j-1-visa-abuse-employers-exploit-foreign-students-under-us-government-program-meant-2216874.

49. **Who's Mr. Holding:** Chris Millspaugh. *Idaho Mountain Express.* June 9, 1977.

50. **There's almost nobody there:** John Briley. "At Sun Valley, crowds are down but skiing's still glorious." *Washington Post.* November 25, 2011. wapo.st/35iNB2g.

51. **roughly 22,000 riders per hour:** "Sun Valley Fun Facts." *Visit Sun Valley.* www.visitsunvalley.com/about-sun-valley/sun-valley-fun-facts/.

52. **fishing and playing golf:** Pat Murphy. July 14, 1999. "Allen & Co bid relaxation goodbye." *Idaho Mountain Express.* archives.mtexpress.com/1999/07-14-99/l14murph.htm.

Five: The Valley – Quality of Life and Quality of Place

53. **unmarred by artificial lighting:** Central Idaho Dark Sky Reserve. idahodarksky.org/.

54. **or brick commercial buildings:** World Population Review. worldpopulationreview.com/us-counties/. The Review is the source of all population numbers in this chapter.

55. **from 365,000 to $392,500:** Express Staff. "Real estate prices continue to rise." *Idaho Mountain Express.* November 22, 2019. bit.ly/3kG4dJP. All housing prices came from the *Idaho Mountain Express.*

56. **small towns in America:** Stefanie Waldek and Elizabeth Stamp. "The 25 Best Small Towns in America." *Architectural Digest.* December 30, 2019.

57. **parallel to the Big Wood River:** Trail Link by Rails to Trails Conservancy. "Wood River Trail History." August 2020. www.traillink.com/trail-history/wood-river-trail/.

58. **who earned roughly $77,353:** Economic Policy Institute. "Income Inequality in Idaho." www.epi.org/multimedia/unequal-states-of-america/#/Idaho.

59. national norm of $62,000: Data USA. "Blaine County, ID." datausa.io/profile/geo/blaine-county-id.

60. increased by nearly $200 million: Alejandra Buitriago. "With sales up, wages remain below the national average." *Idaho Mountain Express.* October 24, 2018. bit.ly/35qcskW.

61. for the average local worker: Zillow. "Blaine County Homes Values." September 30, 2020. www.zillow.com/blaine-county-id/home-values/.

62. solving the housing shortage: Mark Dee. "Cratering wages push Blaine behind state." *Idaho Mountain Express.* May 22, 2019. bit.ly/3pWCZPY.

63. make a reasonable living: Tony Tekaroniake Evans. "Employers: Housing remains a challenge." *Idaho Mountain Express.* December 31, 2019. bit.ly/3zsNJds.

64. wealth that lacked a soul: Carol Black and Neal Marlens. "Lost People of Mountain Village (Part One)," January 22, 2009. www.youtube.com/watch?v=hzoN2MFkCXI. "Lost People of Mountain Village (Part Two)." January 23, 2009. www.youtube.com/watch?v=-1TIeJSUr6I. Also see Nancy Lofholm. "Filmmakers mock luxury of vacancy in Tellride 'burb." *The Denver Post.* February 28, 2006. dpo.st/32gwnBi.

65. a shot of bourbon: Timothy Egan. "Ketchum Journal; Real Life Intrudes On Reverie of The Past." *The New York Times.* August 30, 1999. nyti.ms/2RYnkDj. For another delightful article on Sun Valley, see Timothy Egan. "Sun Valley: An American Original." February 24, 1991. www.nytimes.com/1991/02/24/travel/sun-valley-an-american-original.html?pagewanted=all.

Six: Economic Development Limbo

66. quality of life for a community: International Development Council. www.lakelandtn.gov/DocumentCenter/View/139/What-is-economic-development?bidId=f1.

67. the subject was dropped: Rice Consulting Associates facilitated both retreats.

68. more new homes and businesses: Pat Murphy. "Wood River Valley develops schizophrenic personality." *Idaho Mountain Express.* November 11, 1998. archives.mtexpress.com/1998/11-11-98/murphy11.htm.

69. and managed growth: Alyson Wilson, "WwRAP survey results headed for mailboxes." *Idaho Mountain Express.* November 4-10, 1998. archives.mtexpress.com/1998/11-04-98/wwrapup.htm.

70. we may not be around: Greg Stahl. "Economic mountaineering." *Idaho Mountain Express.* June 23-June 29, 1999. archives.mtexpress.com/1999/06-23-99/localbus.htm.

71. the balance of 43%: Dean Runyan Associates. "Economic Analysis Blaine County, Idaho." Portland, Oregon. May 2001. www.deanrunyan.com.

72. less impacted by the seasons: Strategic Growth Institute for Southern Idaho Economic Development Organization. "Initial Community Planning & Target Industry Recommendations for Blaine County, Idaho." October 2007. www.southernidaho.org/.

73. business development programs: Chuck Wolfe. Claggett Wolfe Associates. "Market Feasibility Study for a Business Incubator in Blaine County, Idaho." August 2010. claggettwolfe.com/#ourprojects.

74. **small business and entrepreneurial growth:** Theory Into Practice Strategies. "An Economic Strategy for Blaine County, Idaho." Austin, Texas. July 2009. tipstrategies.com/.

75. **there is no common vision:** Rebecca Meany. "Consultant rallies chamber on downtown Plans." *Idaho Mountain Express.* January 27, 2006. archives.mtexpress.com/index2. php?ID=2005107686&var_Year=2006&var_Month=01&var_ Day=27.

76. **affordable housing in blighted areas:** Rebecca Meany, "Ketchum looks to Urban Renewal Agency for economic development." *Idaho Mountain Express.* April 5, 2006. bit.ly/3xg8vLs.

77. **a payment schedule or pay-off date:** Greg Stahl. "Councilman to loan URA $1 million." *Idaho Mountain Express.* June 27, 2007. bit.ly/2TABgDZ.

78. **before starting development:** Trevon Milliard. "Putting Ketchum's URA into context. Is there a reason for 5.5 debt?" *Idaho Mountain Express.* October 28, 2009. bit.ly/3gziRPK.

79. **growth in Blaine County:** Peter Jensen. "In Blaine County, a development boom fizzled." *Idaho Mountain Express.* October 7, 2015. bit.ly/3zwmvCH.

80. **restaurant and retail space:** Jon Duval. "Resort files plans for River Run." *Idaho Mountain Express.* Friday, August 14, 2009. archives.mtexpress.com/index2.php?ID=2005127389&var_ Year=2009&var_Month=08&var_Day=14#.WVq3wxXyt0w.

81. **20 years of the urban renewal program:** Trevon Milliard. "Ketchum eyes River Run Taxes." *Idaho Mountain Express.* February 10, 2010. archives.mtexpress.com/ index2.php?ID=2005129984&var_Year=2010&var_ Month=02&var_Day=10#.WnVAy7ynGLs.

82. **likely receive just $10 million-$18 million:** Peter Jensen. "Hotels, economic development will fuel KURA revenues." *Idaho Mountain Express.* April 19, 2017. www.mtexpress.com/news/ketchum/hotels-economic-development-will-fuel-kura-revenues/article_0f0bd4fa-248b-11e7-b4e8-bb387c18cf66. html.

83. **earners in a resort economy:** R.A. Youngman. "Presentation on Sun Valley Resort Area Economy - An Economy Out of Balance." *Sun Valley City Council.* January 2010. The document with relevant background is available at Sun Valley City Hall.

84. **Cleveland of mountain towns:** Our View. "Sun Valley: The Cleveland of mountain towns." *Idaho Mountain Express.* bit. ly/3m0HkA8.

85. **high-end hotels to attract more tourists:** Jim Knight, Jane Fairley, and Bill Wright. "Sun Valley Resort Area 2010 Recommendations." *Sun Valley Independent Marketing Committee.* May 2010. The document with relevant background is available at Sun Valley City Hall.

86. **"Sun Valley" in marketing campaigns:** Trevon Milliard. "Committee: Give 400K more to marketing." May 21, 2010. archives.mtexpress.com/index2.php?ID=2005131436&var_Year=2010&var_Month=05&var_Day=21 65.

87. **Marketing Alliance got the nod:** Trevon Milliard. "Sun Valley reaches boiling point over marketing." September 24, 2010. archives.mtexpress.com/index2.php?ID=2005133389.

88. **affordable housing with public funds:** Trevon Milliard. "URA tries to put affordable housing issue to rest." *Idaho Mountain Express.* April 15, 2011. archives.mtexpress.com/index2. php?ID=2005136198&var_Year=2011&var_Month=04&var_Day=15.

89. **more prominent site:** Starbucks had been on Main Street for a decade, initially denied a permit because one Councilor believed it "would ruin Ketchum's family atmosphere." That same Councilor was the Mayor who, in 2011, pushed for Starbucks on the Town Plaza.

90. **what she could to make it fair**: Trevon Milliard. "URA moves on Starbucks Proposal." *Idaho Mountain Express.* March 18, 2011. archives.mtexpress.com/index2. php?ID=2005135841#.WOVpXUUrJ0w.

91. **lack of coordination and accomplishments:** Katherine Wutz. "Just get it done." *Idaho Mountain Express.* October 1, 2010. http://archives.mtexpress.com/index2.php?ID=2005133486& var_Year=2010&var_Month=10&var_Day=01.

92. **small business and affordable housing development:** For more information on the KCDC, see its website: www.ketchumkcdc.com/.

93. **directors came and went:** Jima Rice. "Evaluate KIC's effectiveness." *Idaho Mountain Express.* July 25, 2018. bit.ly/3a0CtcF

94. **efficiency, and sustainability:** Charity Navigator. "Ketchum Community Development Corporation." www.charitynavigator.org/ein/861175157.

95. **data about its successes:** For more information on SVED see its website: sunvalleyeconomy.com.

96. **problems were identified:** Amy Busek. "Ketchum URA addresses identity crisis." *Idaho Mountain Express.* May 6, 2015. www.mtexpress.com/news/ketchum/ketchum-ura-addresses-identity-crisis/article_7b5b7906-f37a-11e4-a052-8304f8e7a9c2.html.

97. **I've been with the KCDC:** Amy Busek. "Taking a chance on valley living." *Idaho Mountain Express.* May 29, 2015. www.

mtexpress.com/news/ketchum/taking-a-chance-on-valley-living/article_8f758cc0-057b-11e5-9e3a-d3108f17724b.html.

98. **lease agreement with Starbucks:** Express Staff. "Starbucks appraised at $1.5 million. *Idaho Mountain Express.* April 17, 2017. bit.ly/3cIyAf8

Seven: The Case for Entrepreneurs

99. **vibrancy, authenticity, and scenic beauty**: Americans for the Arts. "Arts and Economic Prosperity 5." *AmericansForTheArts.org/AEP5.*

100. **up from 39% in 2018:** Lydia Saad. Gallup. January 5, 2021. news.gallup.com/poll/328268/country-living-enjoys-renewed-appeal.aspx.

101. **dose of localized flavor:** Martin Zwilling. "5 Lessons in Entrepreneurship From Small-Town Startup Experience." *Inc.* January 7, 2019. www.inc.com/martin-zwilling/how-to-start-a-successful-new-business-in-your-local-small-town.html.

102. **and Redmond, Oregon (30,000):** Jenna Temkin. Brookings. "How a rural Virginian town is using entrepreneurship to boost its local economy." August 1, 2019. www.brookings.edu/blog/the-avenue/2019/08/01/how-a-rural-virginian-town-is-using-entrepreneurship-to-boost-its-local-economy/.

103. **population of 523 in 2019.** Jason Duff. "Young Entrepreneurs: All Small Towns Have Multimillion-Dollar Opportunities." *Inc.* www.inc.com/empact/young-entrepreneurs-all-small-towns-have-multi-million-dollar-opportunities.html.

Eight: The Future is Now!

104. **locals together around those goals:** James and Deborah Fallows. *Our Towns: A 100,000 Mile Journey Into the Heart of America.* (New York, New York: Pantheon Books, 2018.)

105. **the local economy prevail:** Editorial Board. "Business needs a Voice." *Idaho Mountain Express.* October 16, 2019. www. mtexpress.com/opinion/editorials/business-needs-a-voice/ article_5508dbee-ef75-11e9-b92a-5b933b98f500.html.

106. **Silicon Valley Couloir in Jackson, Wyoming:** Silicon Couloir. www.siliconcouloir.com/.

107. **National Center for Economic Gardening:** "Economic Gardening: An Entrepreneurial Approach." Technologies include database research, search engine optimization, and geographic information systems to identify new markets, competitors, and industry trends. economicgardening.org/. See also "Seven Steps to Developing an Economic Gardening Implementation Strategy." *International City/County Management Association.* September 16, 2010. icma.org/about-icma.

108. **connect with funding sources:** U.S. Small Business Administration. www.sba.gov/.

109. **support services to entrepreneurs:** Goldman Sachs. 10,000 Small Businesses Initiative. www.goldmansachs.com/ citizenship/10000-small-businesses/US/). Other resources include Gaebler Ventures (www.gaebler.com/.), Main Street America (www.mainstreet.org/about-us), and The Main Street Alliance (www.mainstreetalliance.org/about),

110. **they'll ruin it:** Stuart Elliot, Stuart. "Employing Softest of Sells for a Resort in Sun Valley." *The New York Times.* November 11, 2011. www.nytimes.com/2011/11/07/business/media/ in-ads-for-sun-valley-resort-the-softest-of-sells.html.

111. **products from its competitors:** In some of the marketing campaigns in the last couple of decades, the Valley's brand has been inconsistent and just plain strange. There was "Friedl Pfeiffer" (a ski instructor in Austrian garb hanging in the sky with dangling skis); "Skippy-the Stone" (an online game in

which the player throws a stone toward a watering hole in a cow pasture); and "The Unbeaten Path: It will find you when you're ready" (whatever that means).

112. **find the video on Vimeo:** Lisa Carton. "Small Town, Big Life." 2015. vimeo.com/135295246. The video was nominated for a 2015 Idaho Media Award.

113. **for many of these efforts:** Sun Valley Institute for Resilience. www.sunvalleyinstitute.org/.

114. **considering the idea:** Climate Action Coalition. www.idahoearthguide.com/climate-action-coalition.

115. **little regard for conservation:** In 2015, States at Risk scored 50 states for their climate change preparedness. Idaho's scores were well below average. statesatrisk.org/idaho. For further information, see Sarah Tory. "Is the West Ready for the Impacts of Climate Change?" *High Country News.* December 16, 2015. www.hcn.org/articles/is-the-west-ready-for-the-impacts-of-climate-change?utm_source=wcn1&utm_medium=email.

116. **are more energy efficient:** The Resort's website describes its many efforts for environmental sustainability. www.sunvalley.com/environmental-awareness.

117. **steward of the environment:** National Ski Areas Association. "Endorse Sustainable Slopes." www.nsaa.org/environment/sustainable-slopes/.

118. **same narrow glacial trough:** Kevin Wiser. "Grappling with growth in the Wood River Valley." *Idaho Mountain Express.* December 29, 1999-January 4, 2000. archives.mtexpress.com/1999/12-29-99/growth12-29.htm.

119. **and adjunct care providers:** Emily Jones. "A Blaine County portrait: What demographics tell us." *Idaho Mountain Express.* October 23, 2019. bit.ly/39ZJKJE

Bibliography

Abramson, Rudy. *Spanning the Century: The Life of W. Averell Harriman, 1891-1986.* New York: William and Morrow Company, Inc., 1992.

Belson, Neil A. "Promoting Rural Entrepreneurship and Rural Economic Development." Third Way. January 7, 2020. www.thirdway.org/report/promoting-rural-entrepreneurship-and-rural-economic-development.

Blakely, Edward J. and Nancey Green Leigh. *Planning Local and Economic Development: Theory and Practice.* Thousand Oaks, California: Sage Publications, 2010.

Blanchard, Florence. *Sun Valley Magazine.* October 5, 2010. sunvalleymag.com/articles/hot-springs-hotels/.

Boulton, Guy. "Earl Holding: Maverick entrepreneur has made a fortune through hard work and patience." *The Salt Lake Tribune.* February 2000. archive.sltrib.com/article.php?id=56191172&itype=cmsid.

Brown, Gretchen. "The Benefits of Being a Small-Town Entrepreneur." *REWIRE.* August 23, 2019. www.rewire.org/benefits-small-town-entrepreneur/.

Carman, Zac. "Four Reasons Small Cities Are Better for Big Business." *Forbes.* www.entrepreneur.com/article/290880. May 3, 2017.

Claggett Wolfe Associates. "Market Feasibility Study for a Business Incubator in Blaine County, Idaho." August 2010. claggett-wolfe.com/#ourprojects.

Clifford, Hall. *Downhill Slide: Why the Corporate Ski Industry is Bad for Skiing, Ski Towns, and the Environment.* San Francisco, California: Sierra Club Books. 2002.

Dean Runyan Associates. "Economic Analysis Blaine County, Idaho." Portland, Oregon. Auburn, California. May 2001.

Edwards, Andrew s R. *The Sustainability Revolution: Portrait of a Paradigm Shift.* British Columbia, Canada: New Society Publishers, 2005.

Evans, Tony Tekaroniake. *A history of Indians in the Sun Valley area.* Hailey, Idaho: Blaine County Historical Museum, 2017.

Fallows, James and Deborah. *Our Towns: A 100,000 Mile Journey Into the Heart of America.* New York, New York: Pantheon Books, 2018.

Fox, Porter. *Deep: The Story of Skiing and the Future of Snow.* Jackson Hole, Wyoming: Rink House Productions, 2013.

Friedman, Thomas. *Hot, Flat and Crowded: Why We Need a Green Revolution and How it Can Renew America.* New York, New York: Farrar, Straus and Giroux, 2008.

Gilaberte-Búrdalo, M., F. López-Martín, M. R. Pino-Otín, J. I. López-Moreno. "Impacts of Climate Change on Ski Industry." *ScienceDirect.* 2014. www.sciencedirect.com/science/article/abs/pii/S1462901114001269.

Haeg, Larry. *Harriman vs Hill: Wall Street's Great Railroad War.* Minneapolis, Minnesota: University of Minnesota Press, 2013.

Holland, Wendolyn Spence. *Sun Valley: An Extraordinary History.* Ketchum, Idaho: Idaho Press, 1998.

Howe, Jim, Ed McMahon, and Luther Propst. *Balancing Nature and Commerce in Gateway Communities.* Washington, D.C.: Island Press, 1997.

Isaacson, Walter and Evan Thomas. *The Wise Men: Six Friends and the World They Made.* New York, New York. Simon & Schuster Paperbacks, 1986. Especially Chapters 1-3.

Kroll, Luisa. "Remembering Robert Earl Holding, Billionaire Owner of Sun Valley Ski Resort." *Forbes.* April 22, 2013.

Lundin, John. *Early Skiing on Snoqualmie Pass.* Charleston, S.C.: The History Press, 2017.

Lundin, John. *Images of America: Sun Valley, Ketchum, and the Wood River Valley.* Mount Pleasant, South Carolina: Arcadia Publishing, 2020.

Moon, Garrett. "How 'Small Town' Entrepreneurs Can Use Location to Their Advantage." *Entrepreneur Magazine.* September 29, 2017. www.entrepreneur.com/article/300734.

Moorehead, Caroline. *The Letters of Martha Gellhorn.* New York, New York: Henry Holt and Sons, 2006.

Nash, Roderick Frazier. *Wilderness and the American Mind (Fourth edition).* New Haven: Yale University Press, 1982.

Olson, Lynn. *Citizens of London: The Americans Who Stood with Britain in its Darkest, Finest Hour.* New York, New York: Random House, 2011.

Oppenheimer, Doug and Jim Poore. *Sun Valley: A Biography.* Boise, Idaho: Beatty Books, 1976.

Sauter, Van Gordon. *The Sun Valley Story.* Hailey, Idaho: Mandala Media, 2011.

Smith, Hedrick. *Who Stole the American Dream?* New York: Random House Trade Paperback Edition, 2013.

Smith, Paul. *Clint Eastwood: A Cultural Production.* Minneapolis, Minnesota: University of Minnesota Press, 1993.

Spence, Clark. *Mining History for Wood River or Bust: Idaho's silver boom of the 1880's.* Caldwell, Idaho: University of Idaho Press (the Idaho Legacy Series) and Caxton Press, 1999.

Stangler, Dane. "Small Cities For Entrepreneurs. Can Start-Ups Entrepreneurs Enjoy Big Success In Small Places?" bit.ly/39sxd1r.

Strategic Growth Institute for Southern Idaho Economic Development Organization. "Initial Community Planning & Target Industry Recommendations for Blaine County, Idaho." October 2007.

Sun Valley Independent Marketing Committee. "Sun Valley Resort Area 2010 Recommendations." May 2010.

Taylor, Dorice. *Sun Valley.* Sun Valley, Idaho: Ex Libris, 1980.

TIP Strategies. "An Economic Strategy for Blaine County, Idaho." Austin, Texas. July 2009.

Trimble, Stephen. *Bargaining for Eden: The Fight for the Last Open Spaces in America.* Oakland, California: University of California Press. 2008.

Tuohy, Jennifer. "Schaffgotsch and Harriman." *Sun Valley Guide.* Winter 2011-2012. www.svguide.com/w12/count.php. Winter 2011-2012.

Waters, Steve. "These firms are the engine of small business creation." *SMB Intelligence.* smbintelligence.com/why-prime-growth-most-likely-to-create-new-jobs/. May 10, 2018.

Williams, Colby. *Small Town, Big Money: Entrepreneurship and Opportunity in Today's Small Town. Kindle Edition* 2018. smalltownbook.com.

Youngman, R.A. "Presentation on LOT Revenue to Sun Valley City Council." January 2010. (Available at Sun Valley City Hall).

Youngman, R.A. "Presentation on Sun Valley Resort Area Economy - An Economy Out of Balance" Sun Valley City Council. May 2010. (Available at Sun Valley City Hall).

About the Author

Jima Rice, Ph.D. is a psychologist and business consultant. Since 1982, she has worked with executives, managers, and entrepreneurs in more than 250 public, private, and non-profit organizations. She has an M. Ed. and Ph.D. in psychology, both from Harvard University. Jima has been one of Idaho's Women of the Year and won awards for her newsletter, Jigsaw Business Weekly. She lives in Ketchum, Idaho where she founded the Wood River Economic Partnership, the non-profit Jigsaw, and the Hatchery, a business incubator to help entrepreneurs grow their businesses.

Made in the USA
Middletown, DE
26 November 2021